KAY N. SANECKI

D0417872

Discovering
Herbs

SHIRE PUBLICATIONS LTD

Front cover: *The herb garden at Rosemoor, the Royal Horticultural Society's garden in Devon.*

British Library Cataloguing in Publication Data
Sanecki, Kay N. (Kay Naylor),
Discovering herbs.– 7th ed.– (Discovering ; 89)
1. Herbs 2. Herb gardening
I. Title II. Herbs
641.3'57
ISBN 0 7478 0590 3

ACKNOWLEDGEMENTS
The photographs on pages 27, 38 (top), 47, 52, 57, 58, 69, 77, 78, 81, 82, 90, 98, 104, 106, 107, 115, 122 and 125 are by Sue Ross. All other photographs, including that on the front cover, are by Cadbury Lamb.

Copyright © 1970 and 2004 by Kay N. Sanecki. First published 1970. Second edition 1973; reprinted 1976 and 1978. Third edition, 1982. Fourth edition 1985, reprinted 1988. Fifth edition 1993. Sixth edition 1997. Seventh edition, revised and updated with colour illustrations, 2004. Number 89 in the Discovering series. ISBN 0 7478 0590 3.

Printed in Great Britain by CIT Printing Services Ltd, Press Buildings, Merlins Bridge, Haverfordwest, Pembrokeshire SA61 1XF.

Contents

A place for herbs 5

Growing herbs 7

Harvesting herbs 18

Drying herbs 21

Herbs to grow 25

Cooking with herbs 119

Pot-pourri 123

Herb gardens today 125

National Plant Collections ® in Britain 132

Further reading 134

Index 135

Priest House, West Hoathly, Sussex, where over 150 different herbs grow in the garden.

A place for herbs

To most people the word *herb* seems to conjure up some delight of the palate, almost a mental taste, confused with a sweet aroma. Our forefathers indeed used plants to add flavour, to vary flavour or to mask putrefaction of food, and some herbs are still commonly employed in traditional practices. With regard to their medicinal use the story is somewhat different, for herbalism as such was practised by ancient civilisations and the Anglo-Saxon word *dregen*, to dry, is the source of the word *drug*. Much of our acceptance of the medicinal action of plants is traditional and herbal practice employs the simple methods that have sufficed for generations. The early herbalists were botanists; the early botanists wrote and illustrated the herbals – some of the earliest books to be produced in Europe – and, inevitably, botany and medicine stem from twin courses. The great schism came during the seventeenth and eighteenth centuries when folk remedies were frequently employed alongside the newly established orthodox medicine, and a herbalist was frequently an apothecary or a barber surgeon. The general flow of population towards the town in the nineteenth century meant that many people were deprived of the proximity of their known remedies and clung to the few tried and tested plants available for sale, sometimes under cover, while the traditional remedies were, for the great part, perpetuated among the rural communities. As orthodox medicine developed it drew on traditional knowledge and many established drugs of today are plant products. It is noteworthy that poisonous drug extracts like belladonna, digitalis, aconite and stramonium are employed in orthodox medicine. In the urban communities herbalism became a shadowy cult until its revival at the beginning of the twentieth century, and today there is an ever strengthening interest in the 'natural' remedy.

The English names of plants often suggest the use to which the plant was put in former times, such as throatwort, bladderwort, eyebright, lungwort – the word *wort* meaning plant – and long after the plant had fallen into disuse the name lives on. The specific Latin name *officinalis* means that this is the species employed medicinally, or officially.

Today the greatest interest is taken in herbs for culinary

delight and for their sweet-smelling qualities. There is an undeniable fascination in growing something of old-world charm and association, especially when it can be reinstated in modern guise as a condiment. The English names are used throughout this book; in the chapter 'Herbs to grow' the Latin names are given for clarity of identification. The modern vogue for collecting something – anything it would seem – cannot be more delightfully engaged upon than by making a collection of growing plants that have folklore associations through the centuries and yet provide useful material and interest. Suggestions for growing and using these plants are given in later pages, without any reference to the legends and myths that surround them – these can be sought elsewhere – and the emphasis is on cultivating herbs.

The National Herb Centre at Warmington, Warwickshire.

Growing herbs

The beginner need not be deterred from starting to grow herbs by lack of horticultural know-how or by meagre funds. To attain some measure of success two factors are essential: a suitable soil and some shelter from prevailing winds.

Soil

The first condition is best fulfilled by choosing plants that will either like or tolerate the type of soil rather than by making a sustained effort to change the nature of the soil, and provided that the site is not waterlogged or badly drained some herbs can be grown. A heavy clay soil is the least suitable for herbs, and mint is probably the only culinary herb that can be expected to flourish, but much can be done to ameliorate the condition of such a soil and lighten its texture. This is achieved by the addition of compost, peat or one of its alternatives, and other humus-encouraging materials. A clay soil, well managed, is perfectly suited to the cultivation of herbs. At the other end of the scale a very light sandy, hungry soil also needs humus in the form of compost, peat and leaf mould to improve its moisture-retentive qualities and until this can be achieved only those herbs that flourish in baked soils, like rosemary, marjoram and thymes, can be expected to thrive properly.

Thus, on whatever soil herbs are to be grown, the preparation of the land, to bring it into good heart, is the first essential and time and money used in this way are well spent. Clear perennial weeds by forking out and an application of a residual weed killer in autumn will help to keep the land free of annual weeds the following spring. Lightly fork in compost, or whatever humus-producing material is available during the autumn, and let the hard weather do the remainder of the work.

Compost is derived from vegetable waste, both kitchen scraps and garden material: weeds, potato and pea haulms, lawn mowings, hedge clippings and the like. Layers of this material should alternate with layers of good garden soil and a sprinkling of a proprietary compost activator, to form a compost heap. A bin can be filled in layers and the contents left to rot and break down to a brown crumbly texture for some six months before being forked on to the land to provide organic material.

Organic fertilisers include bonemeal or boneflour, hoof and horn and dried blood, and inorganic fertilisers (strictly the so called 'artificials') are manufactured products of known chemical content usually sold as granules or pellets. In general, herbs do not require the balanced and controlled feeding obtainable from this type of fertiliser except in a few instances where the plant needs a fillip to recover after a crop has been taken.

Shelter

Herbs are always at their best in warm still air and protection from the prevailing winds is essential, although any shelter provided should not plunge the herb border into shade. It is a good idea to plant a herb hedge, of rosemary, sage, artemisia, lavender or roses, and while these are growing some measure of temporary windbreak can be provided quickly by growing annual sunflowers. The long-term plan of growing a hedge to surround a herb garden is justified because the seclusion will prevent drying winds from robbing the plants of their aromatic qualities and a completeness of design will be achieved.

Starting a herb garden

Some herbs are raised annually from seed sown in the early months of the year: chervil, dill, summer savory, basil, caraway, borage, parsley, purslane and corn salad. Seed can be bought cheaply or saved from the previous summer and needs to be sown in March in pots or boxes, thinned, hardened off and planted out of doors in May; or sown directly into the ground in drills during April and May. Summer savory, basil, borage, purslane and corn salad are treated this way. Umbelliferous plants such as chervil, dill, caraway and parsley run to seed if transplanted as seedlings. Make two sowings of such plants as purslane and corn salad to ensure a succession of fresh young leaves. If the drill for parsley is watered with very hot water immediately before sowing the period of germination will be shortened, for parsley seed is notoriously slow to germinate. One or two herbs, notably angelica, verbascum, clary sage, woad and evening primrose, are biennials. That is, they are sown one year, usually in summer, to flower the following one. Several biennials appear to behave like perennials once they are established, especially if the flowering stems are cut away and the plants are not allowed to form seed. Other plants, like borage, marigolds and fennel, sow themselves so easily that their effect is perennial.

Parsley used as edging at Hatfield House in Hertfordshire.

Most of the perennial herbs, such as chicory, comfrey and lemon balm, can also be raised from seed although vegetative propagation from divisions, offsets or cuttings is sometimes less hazardous. Tarragon, chives, marjoram and mint can be divided easily in spring. Cuttings of rosemary, lavender and santolina can be struck, in a frame, in spring or, if made with a heel of old wood, in the open, in July. (This involves tearing away a small strip of the old wood at the base of the cutting, so that a sprig of the present season's growth has a tag of last year's growth attached to it.) Put cuttings into a sandy compost in a box, frame or open land and protect them from sunshine. Young roots will form soon in most cases and the rooted cuttings can be planted out in the autumn or the following spring.

In the chapter 'Herbs to grow' each plant is described as annual, biennial or perennial to guide the amateur in the general pattern of their cultivation and propagation.

Renovating an old herb garden

Worn-out or scraggy plants are best thrown out, and after the ground has been forked over and cleared of creeping roots and perennial weeds a fresh supply of plants can be sown or planted.

Lavender bushes that have become leggy and bare need to be grubbed out and rooted cuttings can be planted out to replace them, but where sage or thyme has grown straggly build up a mound of good garden soil or potting compost around them, making it firm and leaving only the tips of the shoots protruding. Roots will form quite quickly along the covered stems at the leaf joints and these shoots can be severed and replanted tidily, and the old foundation plants discarded. Frequently a neglected herb garden looks much worse than it need because the hedges have become overgrown or unproductive at the base. Rose hedges can be cut right back to within a few inches of the ground and will break again, and box and santolina can be clipped right back with sharp shears. The new leafy growth will soon thicken up the hedge.

Many of the larger nurseries stock the generally cultivated herbs, and some garden centres have plentiful supplies in the spring. But there are good nurseries that specialise in herbs and herb products from which the more unusual plants and collector's items can be purchased. There is also a growing number of seedsmen specialising in wild flower, old vegetable and herb seeds; their catalogues make exciting reading. It is always advisable to obtain either plants or seed from a reliable source and any herb nursery or farm that is a member of the British Herb Traders Association can be relied upon to provide good clean stock. Furthermore, for the most part, they have the plants properly identified.

Many herbs are native to Europe, including Britain, and there is perhaps a temptation to collect plants from the wild. Under the Conservation of Wild Creatures and Wild Plants Act, 1975, it is an offence for anyone, without permission of the owner or occupier of the land, to dig up plants in the countryside. This refers to any wild plant, not just the twenty-one scheduled species which are totally protected by the Act.

What to grow

The selection of plants to include in a herb garden is a personal decision depending on site, available space and requirements.

Culinary herbs such as a cook might prefer to include are mint, sage, parsley, chives, basil, tarragon, caraway, rosemary,

Nasturtium is a colourful addition to the herb garden.

lovage and salad crops like dandelion, nasturtium and corn salad. Only a small number of plants is needed for such a collection because only a few leaves at a time are gathered unless the plants are to be dried and stored for winter use, in which case more will be required.

Decorative herbs can be assembled in a more extensive collection, to include a representative array wherein the officinal, culinary and decorative plants of old-world association can be grown together. Here one could include tansy, rosemary, roses, bergamot, catmint, foxglove, lily-of-the-valley, poppy, sunflower and many others.

Medicinal herbs or herbs of healing would include many wild flowers, as these were the first simples known to our ancestors and some such as coltsfoot should be introduced with care as they can be invasive. Sink an old bucket or plastic bowl and plant these wandering types in it to waylay the travelling rootstocks and confine the growth without too much hard work. Selfheal, pulmonaria, raspberry, horehound, coltsfoot, hyssop, comfrey, foxglove, feverfew and agrimony would each merit inclusion in a medicinal collection.

Sweet-smelling herbs for the scented garden can be classified in two ways: those that give off their perfume into the air or some that need the merest brush of the hand to encourage them to loosen their aroma; and those that are less generous and need to be crushed or bruised to release their scent. Many cottage garden plants fall into the first category: pinks, wallflowers, lilac, daphne, honeysuckle, stocks, narcissi, violets, lily-of-the-valley, heliotrope and roses. Among those that need encouragement to exhale their perfume are tansy, nasturtium, marigold, thyme, chamomile, box, pelargonium, rosemary, lavender, rue, mint, salvia, bergamot and artemisia.

A natural order garden probably appeals to the gardener of botanical inclination, each bed housing plants within the same natural order. These can be interesting but are of insignificant decorative value. The plants belonging to, say, *Labiatae*, such as salvia, rosemary, marjoram and hyssop, can be grouped together and in another bed the compositous plants such as coltsfoot, chicory and sunflower. The *Umbelliferae* collection would include fennel, dill, caraway and parsley. In the chapter 'Herbs to grow' the natural order of each plant is recorded not only for the purpose of description but to guide the beginner with ideas for making such a collection.

Planning the herb garden

The size of the herb plot, be it kitchen border or extensively decorative garden, is again a matter of personal taste and depends largely upon the space and funds available, but the decision of long or short term planting has to be reached at the outset. Assuming one plant is allowed per square foot as a general guide, on richer soils a matured effect can be achieved in two or three years, while on the drier soils this rate of planting will give a more sparse result and will need up to four years for effect.

Borders. The less sophisticated the herb border, the better. Plants need to be assembled in groups where the texture or shape of the leaves of one kind will act as a foil for those of its neighbour, in much the same way as a herbaceous border is planned. The lower-growing plants, say thyme, chives, violets, and marigolds, need to be set towards the front of the border, the taller ones, like angelica, mullein and sage, to the back. Some form of background is necessary. If it is provided by a wall, then roses, jasmine or honeysuckle can be trained over it; or shrubs or a hedge can form the background. Roses, bay, the rough-leaved sage and box are all suitable. Refrain from the temptation of using privet or elder as the background hedge; while both grow rapidly and provide flowers redolent in their season, they will impoverish the border by their foraging roots.

The border can be planned formally, setting the plants either in rectangular blocks or in wedge-shaped sections arranged fanwise. In both instances the proportions are important and, for attractive results, the border should be fairly wide and not a long narrow strip of ground.

Formal designs. No one would describe herbs as first-class plants where good garden effect is required and thus by using them in a repeated theme complemented by the bold design of formal-shaped beds the best herb gardens are designed. Based upon either a circle or a rectangle of varying proportions, a series of interesting plants can be evolved. The simplest is to imitate the rim and spokes of a wheel, marking them out in box, santolina or pinks, and to fill the 'wedges' between each spoke with contrasting plants. The central hub of the wheel can be emphasised by a sundial, birdbath, seat, beehive or standard plant, such as a rose or honeysuckle. Essentially, the 'wheel' must not be too small.

Planned along straight lines, rather than curves or arcs, the square or rectangular enclosed garden lends itself best as a herb or aromatic garden. Beds should be large enough not to give a dotted effect and yet small enough to be workable. Perhaps the edges can be traced in some plant such as pinks, santolina, lavender or box, related to the size of the bed itself

The circular herb bed in the Herb Society's garden at Sulgrave Manor.

The thyme pavement in the herb garden of the Royal Horticultural Society's garden at Rosemoor in Devon.

and to the garden in general. Individual beds can be planned to hold a number of herbs, each of which ought to be planted in more than one bed to bring the design together as a whole. Or the individual beds could be planted entirely with one plant or one group of plants – culinary, dye, medicinal, folklore, still room, strewing or nosegay. Another idea is to confine plants of a coloured foliage into one bed, say silver-grey leaved plants such as some artemisias, lavender cotton, lavender, sage, curry plant, mullein, camphor plant, eucalyptus, horehound, sea holly and thymes such as *Thymus* x *citriodorus* 'Silver Queen' and *Thymus vulgaris* 'Silver Posie'. Dark or purple-leaved plants could be collected together; they would be fennel in the bronze-shaped form, the purple sage, peppermint, wall germander, basil 'Dark Opal', black horehound and juniper.

The chequerboard design is a favourite for a herb collection, where small square beds are formed in staggered rows, each devoted to an individual plant. The same theme can be used less formally where patches of herbs are tucked into spaces between the paving stones of a patio or terrace and to good

*The chequerboard design in the herb garden of the University of
Liverpool Botanic Garden at Ness on the Wirral.*

effect if the thymes, pennyroyal, mints and chamomile are
used, as they emit their fragrance when crushed underfoot. A
pavement or path garden can be used to cover a large or small
area, thus providing a useful thoroughfare in the garden and
at the same time a near trouble-free herb garden.

The most elaborately designed herb garden is one made
along the lines of an Elizabethan knot garden and based upon
an intricate pattern of beds, each outlined by clipped box or
santolina. Designs can vary from rectangular beds to intricate
decorative curves emulating the outline of leaves, but the
constant factor is that the design is repetitive and is intended
to be regarded as a whole and from above or afar to be
enjoyed as a parterre.

Where more extensive gardens are planned a carefully
selected tree or trees can be included. Suggestions are rowan,
mulberry, magnolia, calycanthus, lime, witch hazel,
eucalyptus, elder or bay.

Growing herbs in confined spaces

Not everyone who wishes to cultivate a few herbs has a
garden or even space to spare in the garden, but many herbs,
particularly the culinary ones, are accommodating in that
they will thrive in confined root runs and so can be expected

to grow quite happily in tubs, pots and window-boxes.

Innumerable gardens simply do not have appropriate areas where herbs can be cultivated, lacking light or shelter or perhaps having only a heavy soil. By cultivating herbs and aromatic plants in containers, they can be moved to a sunny spot or taken elsewhere once their most interesting season is over. Pots can be sunk into a border, to rim level, and changed from time to time according to how the plants are doing and what else in the garden is in flower.

Containers can be troughs, window-boxes, tubs, hanging baskets, pots or even a purpose-built low wall, of brick or stone, where plants can be grown along the top. Such a wall is a most acceptable edge to a patio or acts as a division between one part of the garden and another. Where herbs are to be grown in any of these ways it is a good idea to consider them only as summer plants, using the containers for something else like bulbs or spring bedding plants at other periods of the year. The trick is to plant rooted cuttings of herbs into the containers, or those little plants that can be purchased from garden centres, their roots encased in black plastic bags. Containers should be filled with compost, and the small plants tucked in. Move the arrangement of bags around before actually planting so that a pleasing assembly results. Be prepared to remove any plant that outgrows the proportions of its container or grows out of proportion with its neighbours, for the trick of container-grown herbs is to plant closely and treat them as though they are intended to be temporary residents. Remember that during warm weather containers of all kinds need watering.

Some suggestions are:

Troughs: thymes, chives, rooted cuttings of bay, rosemary and chamomile.

Window-boxes: basil, especially 'Dark Opal', bay, chives, corn salad, feverfew, lavender cotton, lungwort, marjoram, nasturtium, parsley, rue, tarragon and thymes.

Tubs: bay, chives, feverfew, lavender cotton, lungwort, nasturtium, parsley, lavender, rosemary, tarragon, wall germander, artemisias, lemon balm, hyssop, fennel, mint and sage.

Indoors: lemon verbena, pineapple sage, parsley, rosemary, marjoram, bush basil (especially in autumn when it has finished in the garden), thymes, mint (in water) and chives.

In walls: catmint, chamomile, feverfew, horehound, lungwort, rue, marjoram, thymes, houseleek, sea holly, lavender cotton, curry plant, sages, especially the purple and tricolor forms, hyssop, savories and marigolds.

Hanging baskets: thyme, nepeta, alchemilla, rosemary (rooted cuttings), sage (rooted cuttings), marjoram, savory, mint (especially apple mint and where there is shade), lungwort and feverfew.

A hop-covered arbour in the herb garden of the Royal Horticultural Society's gardens at Wisley in Surrey.

Harvesting herbs

Having grown the herbs, it is essential to know which part of the plant is required – leaves, seeds or root – and when it is ready for harvesting. Information as to the part of the plant used is easily acquired but knowing exactly when to harvest to advantage takes a little practical experience. The general rule for cutting leaves is to do so just as the flowers come to be fully opened, because this is the apogee of the plant's annual metabolism and the active principle in the herb is at its strongest at this time. Roots and seeds should be taken on maturity. It is important to collect the right part of the plant because the active elements are not necessarily present in other parts of the same plant and indeed there are some instances where one part of the plant may be edible and another poisonous: for example, the tubers of the potato are staple food, but the fruits are poisonous.

Roots

Roots need to be lifted carefully with a garden fork or flat-tined potato fork and rubbed or washed free of soil. Autumn is the time to lift roots, when the top growth begins to die back, for then the roots are mature.

Leaves

Individual leaves can be taken from such culinary plants as mint, sage, parsley, rosemary, basil and bay as and when required; or whole young shoots can be removed without detriment to the plant. But to remove a crop of leaves for drying and preserving for winter use is an operation of greater importance and needs subtle timing. Pick whole shoots without rendering an individual plant incapable of carrying on its normal function of flowering or seeding – unless of course the plants are being cleared and have been grown solely for the supply of this season's harvest of leaves. The leaves that are gathered need to be free of insects and disease and dry, and often a gentle shake early in the day will rid them of dew quite quickly and hasten the completely dry condition. The most satisfactory stage at which to collect leaves is just as the flowers are coming to maturity.

Flowers

As soon as a flower is fully open it is at its best. Its colour and perfume are then strongest and the petals unblemished. More of the essential oils can be captured at this time and if lavender and rosemary flowers can be collected the day before they are fully open, so much the better, as the colour will persist more certainly, but only the practised eye can recognise this stage. It is very important that bruising of petals and crushing of flowerheads is avoided.

Whole herb

In some instances all the above-ground parts of a plant are cut and this is usually carried out when the plant is about to flower because it is then at maximum efficiency and at its most useful as an active herb. Sometimes several cuttings are required and some can be taken before the first flowering and others later in the season when secondary bushy growth has been produced as a direct result of the first harvesting. Sage, savory and marjoram can be treated in this way. Secateurs can be used, though the operation is necessarily slow, and where a

The grey-green leaves of sage should be dried before use.

fair quantity of the crop is to be gathered a sharp linoleum knife is a most effective tool and can be used to slash the plant cleanly right back to older growth. Bushy plants like sage, thyme and rosemary can be neatly cut back to the previous year's growth and the work can proceed fairly quickly because the fresh young growth is quite soft and easily cut away. Knives used for this purpose must be kept sharp not only for effectiveness but to prevent tearing the growth.

Seed

Sometimes seed is collected for use and at other times for propagation to maintain stocks of the plants the following year. When it is destined for sowing it should be allowed to ripen as far as possible and be collected only from typical well grown plants. When seed is being taken from plants for culinary use, for example from dill or caraway, the plants can be pulled up and hung upside down with a paper bag tied over the old flowerhead to catch the seeds as they fall from the dried placenta. Do not be tempted to use plastic bags for this purpose, easier though it may be to be able to keep an eye on progress. Porous paper bags are far more likely to preserve the precious harvest. It is sometimes difficult to judge the time at which seed will be ready – a couple of hot days encourage the plant to scatter its seeds seemingly prematurely. Muslin bags popped over the whole inflorescence and tied with string or rubber bands will catch the escaping seeds, and later the stem can be cut below the neck of the bag and the seeds emptied on to paper indoors. Often holidays or periods away from the garden coincide with the time of ripening seeds and by covering the seed heads with paper bags many otherwise elusive seeds can be collected. Seed being saved for propagation needs to be carefully labelled and stored in a cool dry shaded place in paper bags, pill boxes or envelopes of aluminium foil.

Bark

Occasionally the bark contains the active element of the plant and is used especially to provide some plant alkaloids and dyes. Homeopathic medicine usually indicates at what time of the year bark ought to be collected from the various trees and shrubs recognised as drug plants, and it is usually in the spring or autumn that the bark must be carefully shaved off the branches and dried. Collecting bark from trees growing in the wild is not to be encouraged, and great patches of branch should never be left bare or the tree will suffer.

Drying herbs

Drying is the most important operation in the successful culture of herbs and the time and expense of careful cultivation can be forfeited in a matter of hours if the drying process is inadequately or inefficiently carried out. Much of the value of the plant can be lost by hurried or ineffective drying, and for medicinal purposes, certainly, there ought to be a minimum accepted amount of the active alkaloid or glucodine in a given sample of dried material. No herb can be stored fresh; a few can be preserved for culinary use by deep freezing (see later), but the material can be utterly valueless unless it is carefully dealt with after harvesting.

The housewife who wishes to keep a few sprigs of mint, sage, rosemary, chervil, basil, bay and tarragon for winter use can dry freshly collected leaves in a constantly warm airing cupboard, spare bedroom, airy loft or garden shed in open boxes or on sheets of paper, but for any quantity in excess of the small domestic requirements special facilities are necessary. Avoid using kitchens and bathrooms as there is normally too much moisture in the air from cooking and washing. Plants such as sage and thyme can be hung from rafters or on cords stretched across a dry, dust-free room. The bunches should be composed of a few sprigs only and fastened loosely by the stems to allow air to circulate.

An empty greenhouse or a section of the greenhouse screened off by plastic sheeting hung as a temporary partition can provide good conditions. Shade should be given by blinds or a fly sheet or even by sheets of newspaper. Soil beds in the greenhouse need covering with plastic sheeting to prevent the evaporation of moisture from the soil and the ventilation needs to be controlled to maintain a buoyant atmosphere.

A clean wooden garden shed or summer-house can be used for drying small quantities of herbs but one is dependent then upon sun heat, and the natural fluctuation in temperature with the consequent change in moisture content of the atmosphere discourages even drying.

Drying sheds

Where anything other than a small quantity of material is to be dried it is necessary to provide a sufficiently warm atmosphere with adequate heat and ventilation to maintain dryness in spite of the water being drawn off from the plant material. In addition to this, enough space is required to deal with the bulk of material likely to be harvested at any one time, and some means of providing shade from the daylight is needed. Herbs tend to be bleached when dried in sunlight. A drying room is something to consider if one is dealing with herbs in any quantity or engaged in the cultivation of herbs for market when quality is important.

Some form of heating is required, capable of maintaining an equable temperature of 32C (90F), and some form of ventilation to keep the air moving. Water vapour is present in air; the warmer the air the more moisture it can contain and this must be moved away because the faster that dry air can be brought to the plant material the more evenly will the material dry. An extractor fan set high in the room often provides the solution. A common mistake for beginners to make is to introduce freshly gathered plant material into a warm room where herbs are almost dry. The initial moisture drawn from the fresh material is reabsorbed by the dry herbs from the atmosphere. If new material has to be brought into the room before the process has been completed it should be placed high up in the room and for this reason, as well as to be economical of space, plant material is best dealt with in trays stacked in racks. The trays themselves can be made from wooden frames with a cross-piece set in each corner to prevent twisting, over which hessian, butter muslin, old terylene curtains or old sheets are stretched and secured by drawing pins. The trays should be of a size not too unwieldy to handle and can be slung on a series of 'hammocks' set across the room or slotted into racks used for the purpose. Naturally, if racks are used these will determine the dimensions of the trays. Permanent shelving is not advisable because air must be able to circulate around the trays. It is always wise to have all the racks and trays the same size so that trays can be changed from one position in the room to another easily and efficiently.

Drying

It is wise to harvest only the quantity of clean material that can be dealt with the same day and to label each kind of herb carefully to avoid confusion once they are dried; and always keep one plant separate from another. The material should be spread out quite thinly on the trays and during the first two days turned frequently. Get the room sufficiently warm before harvesting and the initial high temperature during the first twenty-four hours of the drying process needs to be 32-34C (90-95F) to reduce the water content of the plant as quickly as possible before any deterioration starts. The moisture content of most plants is well above seventy per cent and the aim is brisk drying without shrivelling, to change the condition of the leaf rather than its chemical content. As the water content is relatively high a considerable bulk of fresh material is needed to provide an adequate supply of the dried product. A broad estimate is that 8 kilos of freshly harvested plant material will provide 1 kilo of dried herb.

After the first twenty-four hours, the temperature can be reduced to 25 or 27C (75 or 80F) to finish off the process evenly without blackening the leaves. The whole process usually takes three to six days. Dryness can be judged by breaking stems between the finger and thumb, and when the process is complete they should snap crisply. Roots need to be tested with a knife and need to be dry right through; if a spongy core remains they will soon rot. Should the drying process be incomplete, moisture will be reabsorbed from the atmosphere, the herbs will smell musty and will soon be mouldy.

Rubbing down

As soon as the herbs are dry and have cooled down some arrangement must be made to store them and, if they are destined for sale, to transport them. Sacks should not be stacked on the floor but are better hung to allow the free movement of air around them. The rubbing-down process needs to be done in good ventilation, probably wearing gloves and certainly a mask as protection against the dust produced during the operation. Domestic amounts of material can be dealt with satisfactorily by hand-picking the leaves, discarding the stalks and crushing the leaves first with a rolling pin and subsequently rubbing them through a fine sieve. Larger quantities may need to be milled in a coffee grinder or domestic mixer once the stalks and chaff have been removed by hand. It is at this stage that one discovers that the leaves were sandy or dirty before drying! For even larger amounts some form of chaff cutter is used but most herbs can be marketed whole after drying, and to deal with these large quantities is a commercial concern.

Storing herbs

The amounts of most domestic preserves are gauged to provide a continuous supply throughout the winter, and herbs are no exception. There is little point in storing large quantities, although attractively packed samples make useful Christmas presents.

Label each kind of herb and store it in some airtight container so that it cannot reabsorb moisture from the atmosphere. Small glass jars with screw tops can be used but ought to be kept in a cupboard away from the light. Wooden boxes or decorative wooden drums make a pleasing alternative. For a short period of time plastic bags may be used, sealed either by using a warm iron or with the wire and paper strips provided with the bags to keep them as airtight as possible. Never use tins for dried herbs.

Freezing

Most culinary herbs can be frozen reasonably satisfactorily, although naturally they are not crisp and fresh when they are brought out and therefore not as useful for garnishing. Those that are floppy or filmy of foliage, such as dill or fennel, are best mixed with other herbs in a suitable combination before freezing, so that they can be used together: say, dill with parsley and chives, for use in sauces: or tarragon and chervil, to flavour egg dishes.

Cut the sprigs of herbs when they are dry, and take only a small amount at a time. Wash them free of grit if necessary and dry thoroughly, then pack in freezer bags and label clearly. Alternatively, freeze small sprigs of flavouring herbs in ice cubes and store, then add to stews and casseroles immediately from the freezer while cooking is in progress. A more reliable method of preservation for most herbs is to blanch quickly before freezing, that is to dip them into boiling water for just a minute before putting into the freezer bags. The satisfactory freezer life for herbs that have been blanched is five or six months. It is less for herbs that have not been blanched.

Herbs to grow

The following catalogue of herbs includes suggestions for various types of collections of herbs. Notes are given as to whether the plant is annual or perennial to provide a guide to cultivation. Some plants included are poisonous and the need to educate children to recognise them cannot be overstressed.

Agrimony

Agrimonia eupatoria (Rosaceae)   Perennial
Yellow agrimony, church steeples

Agrimony is a common hedgerow plant all over Britain, especially on porous soils where it can find a sun-baked spot. The pretty fern-like leaves make a tisane, when infused, fragrant of apricots. The whole plant is faintly aromatic (even the root, especially in spring) and retains the fragrance when dried. The tiny yellow flowers are massed on a slender spike, the lower flowers blooming first, and have earned the plant the country name of church steeples. They are in flower from July onwards, until the cool days come.

The whole plant yields a yellow dye, rather pale from late summer plants, but deepening as the weeks pass in the autumn. Propagation is from seed, which is available from nurseries and seedsmen specialising in wild plants.

Alchemilla

Alchemilla vulgaris (Rosaceae)   Perennial
Lady's mantle, dewcup

A good softening ground cover plant for the front of the herb border, lady's mantle is grown for its legendary protective properties. It is not a herb of the ancient world but one that gained recognition in the magic minded medieval world because of the manner in which the 'magic dew' collects on the leaves. This became part of many a mystic potion. The prettily folded nine-lobed leaves with their distinctive picot edge earn the plant the vernacular name of lady's mantle – turn the leaf over and see how it falls into the folds of a cloak.

The leaves are astringent, and when used as an infusion

are reputed to relieve headaches, especially those accompanying menstruation and general menopausal discomforts, by prolonged use. It will seed itself if allowed to do so and can become persistent quite quickly. Propagation is from spring-sown seed or by division.

Alecost

Tanacetum balsamita (Compositae)   Perennial
Costmary

The plant is commonly confused with the camphor plant (*q.v.*) but the main distinguishing feature is that costmary or alecost has yellow button flowers in July and August, whereas the flowers of the camphor plant are white and daisy-like.

The leaves are ovate, green and a little glaucous and when pressed or crushed they emit a soft balsam-mint aroma. A trace, chopped in a salad, adds a subtle flavour, or the leaves can be added, with restraint, to pot-pourri, because they hold their scent well on drying. It is a plant for a sunny spot, raised from spring-sown seed or propagated by division of roots in spring.

Alexanders

Smyrnium olusatrum (Umbelliferae)   Perennial
Alisanders, black lovage, black pot herb

The whole plant has a yellowish green appearance. The mop heads of flowers resemble those of angelica so strongly that sometimes the two plants are confused. But this plant grows wild in coastal areas, particularly in the south-west of England, and is noticeable early in the season, especially in April, for its lush pale growth which seems so far in advance of all other plants. The stout stems quickly reach a metre or more in height and, when young, afford a celery-flavoured addition to casseroles and soups. The flowers are fragrant, and the leaves large, shining and deeply divided.

Allium

see Garlic

Allspice

Calycanthus floridus (Calycanthaceae)   Tree or shrub

This tree of small proportions bears in August curious

brownish crimson flowers that resemble little bunches of ribbons because the petals are strap-shaped. Every part of the tree is aromatic, rich and spicy. Although this is not a herb, it makes a very attractive and fragrant addition to a sheltered herb garden. Flowers, bark and wood can be included in small amounts in pot-pourri.

Native to the southern United States, this plant is not the source of commercial allspice, which comes from the berries of an evergreen tree native to the West Indies, Central and South America and which is most prolifically grown in Jamaica and has come to be called Jamaica pepper.

Angelica
Angelica archangelica (Umbelliferae)   Perennial

Botanically angelica is a biennial, but seedlings make slow progress the first summer, sometimes flowering the second or third year after sowing and dying after flowering.

Robust flowerheads of angelica.

But the plants sow their seed about the garden, so once introduced angelica will always be at home. Where plants are prevented from flowering and are used for their attractive stalks, they will tend to live on. This is a pity because their large many-spoked mop-head flowers from June to September are a dramatic feature of any garden. So it is necessary to decide to what purpose angelica is to be put in the garden.

Cultivated mainly for its young green stems, which can be candied and used in confectionery, it is a marvellous plant for the back of the border or for a corner, where height is needed. Provide it with some shelter from the wind, so that it can give of its best. Medium damp good garden loam is suitable, where there is shade at some time of the day or day-long dappled shade.

Grow from spring-sown seed, or transplant self-sown seedlings to a salient position in May.

Anise

Pimpinella anisum (Umbelliferae)   Annual

Anise is a dainty half-hardy annual plant, with feathery leaves and tiny white flowers in summer. Its round aromatic seed, well known for flavouring liqueurs, medicine and confectionery, will ripen sufficiently in Britain only in good summers and where the plants are grown in warm sheltered localities. Cut down the whole plant as soon as the seed is ripe and allow it to dry off lying on newspaper in a warm dry dust-free place, so that the seed will fall. In temperate climates the seed does not get a sufficiently long growing season, so for good culinary use it is best to purchase it. Aniseed is one of the best known digestive herbs, and the flavour is sweetly penetrating and licorice-like. Try adding just a drop of an anise-flavoured drink, such as Pernod or Ricard, to a sauce or to garlic butter to serve with shellfish. The Romans took sweetmeats strongly flavoured with anise after rich food, and the seed can be nibbled to sweeten the breath.

Artemisia

see Mugwort, Southernwood, Tarragon and Wormwood

Balm

see Lemon balm and Bergamot

Sweet basil.

Basil, Sweet

Ocimum basilicum (Labiatae)   Annual

It is not easy to get a good crop of basil in damp British summers and it is best treated as a half-hardy annual in most areas of the British Isles. Unfortunately, well established plants seem to lose the sweetness of aroma and take on a strong, rather minty-clove overtone. So the cook who knows and likes to use basil is well advised to try to maintain a supply of young plants for use in the kitchen. It loses much of its interest and unique flavour when dried but is sometimes stored by soaking leaves in good quality olive oil, packing them into a wide-necked jar, with a sprinkling of sea salt, and then filling up the jar with oil. Alternatively, a few leaves can be kept in the freezer, after being painted over with olive oil on both sides.

Sweet basil, sometimes called common basil, has larger leaves than the dwarf, bush basil (*Ocimum minimum*). The latter may be slightly hardier and can certainly be potted up at the end of the summer and grown on indoors to provide autumn leaves for the kitchen. Where frame space is available in the kitchen garden, try growing both basils there. Basil has a great affinity for tomatoes, aubergine and pâté and can be used with restraint to enhance such dishes, for those who like its clove-like flavour.

Bay

Laurus nobilis (Lauraceae)   Tree or shrub
Sweet bay

An evergreen, enjoying a warm sheltered site, bay forms a small tree when left to its own devices, but it is frequently clipped into formal shapes and cultivated in a tub. Cold winds are its principal enemy, searing the aromatic leaves. It is quite difficult to propagate, but seed can be sown in April, or layers of established plants pegged down in summer, or cuttings of young wood taken at the same period and encouraged in a small propagator or frame. The foliage sprigs dry easily when hung up in a warm atmosphere and a leaf may be used, dry or fresh, to flavour casseroles or fish dishes.

Bay.

Bergamot

Monarda didyma (Labiatae)   Perennial
Bee balm, sweet-scented balm, Oswego tea, balm

Originally bergamot came from the swamp areas of North America, and this hints at the conditions it prefers. Sunny moist places suit it best, but where the soil is dry it requires some shade during the day. The red flowers are held around the stem in sparkler fashion and are spiky lipped. They lend a particularly decorative air when used to garnish salads or fruit dishes. As garden plants, cultivars with variously coloured flowers are available, mauve, pink and white, in addition to the handsome reds. The foliage is aromatic and, dried well, can be infused as a pleasant tea.

Betony

Stachys officinalis (Labiatae)   Perennial
Wood betony

Long ago betony was valued as a protection against witches and magical rituals. A northern European native plant of hedgerows and open woodland, in the garden it needs dappled shade or protection from the fiercest noonday sun to give of its best. The short woody rhizomes help it to spread, but not too quickly for the herb border, and the deeply veined dark bright green leaves with their distinctive rounded even teeth (an identifying factor) give a wholesome appearance, and are topped by reddish purple flowers held in a terminal bottle-brush head which seem to stand proudly.

The dried leaves, used as an infusion, are reputed to relieve headaches, or when incorporated into herbal tobacco mixtures are thought to relieve bronchitis. Dried leaves, crushed, may be used also as an ingredient of snuff. Do not use the root or fresh leaves for these remedies. However, leaves may be used fresh to rub on bites or stings to give relief.

Bistort

Polygonum bistorta (Polygonaceae)   Perennial
Snakeroot, Easter ledges

Extensive colonies of bistort are to be found in the north of England and in Scotland, in areas where the plant was mainly used in Easter pudding recipes. It bears rather

Bistort.

weedy, deep pink flowerheads with a straggling habit. Cultivated forms have sugar-pink fat flowerheads from June to August. The twisted black-skinned roots are rich in tannic acid and highly astringent and can be used to stanch bleeding of wounds. Powdered root is used for this purpose. If 250 grams of root is boiled in water for about ten minutes the decoction makes an effective mouthwash or gargle. As a vegetable the leaves in early spring are spinach-like and were used along with young nettle leaves, blackcurrant leaves and parsley, mixed with barley and oatmeal and boiled in a pudding cloth. Later egg and butter were added to make an Easter pudding.

Bloodroot

Sanguinaria canadensis (Papaveraceae)   Perennial
   This is an early spring flowering plant, and the large

palmate lobed leaves develop later in the season. The waxen white flowers have a cluster of golden anthers at the centre. But it is for the root that the plant is grown. It yields an orange-red dye used by the American Indians for painting their skins, and it imparts a similar colour to cloth. It is a poisonous plant and has been used in the treatment of chronic skin disorders such as varicose ulcers. Select a gravel soil for it, if possible where there is dappled shade.

Bog myrtle

Myrica gale (Myricaceae)   Perennial
Sweet gale

The bog myrtle is a native plant of boggy ground, particularly fragrant during warm spells. It is quite difficult to establish but will flourish in acid boggy swampland where all other plants fail. It is well worth trying on the borders of a bog garden or planted in some old container, which can be kept soggy, sunk into a border. The plant may be divided in spring, once it starts to grow. It forms a close bush some 60 cm high and bears inconspicuous flowers. A spice made from the ground dried leaves can be used as flavouring for sauces and gravies and for risotto.

The wax myrtle, *Myrica cerifera*, is a North American evergreen shrub and the glaucous wax which encrusts the bluish fruits that cling to the stems can be made into fragrantly burning candles. For this reason it is sometimes known as candleberry. The foliage yields a yellow dye.

Borage

Borago officinalis (Boraginaceae)   Annual

A hardy annual, the entire borage plant is rough with white, somewhat prickly hairs, which lend a frostiness of appearance. Flowers are a clear azure blue, with prominent black anthers in a central cone. The little ring of blue petals can be slipped away and used to garnish salad or fruit drinks – or even strung together as necklaces to amuse little girls. They may also be candied. A fresh cucumber-like fragrance is emitted from the whole plant, and it can be used to flavour cooling drinks or the leaves can be chopped and added to salads. The herbalist John Parkinson (1567-1650) recommended the borage to expel pensiveness and melancholy.

Borage.

Select a sunny spot or one that at least gets a good deal of sunshine during the day and where there is a well drained soil. Seed can be sown from April to July, although it will seed itself quite satisfactorily after the first season in the garden.

Brooklime

Veronica beccabunga (Scrophulariaceae)　　　　Perennial
Water pimpernel, becky leaves, horse cress

The soft thick leaves of brooklime are generally found growing together with watercress and the two may be eaten together. Brooklime is palatable only when young but its sprawling stems with flat rounded leaves are studded along their length with tiny pale blue flowers in May and June. The entire plant shines and is quite decorative for a boggy area, stream bank or even a tiny damp herb garden made in a container. The juice, combined with that of scurvy grass (*Cochlearia officinalis*) and Seville oranges, was used to form the 'spring juices' formerly valued as a remedy for scurvy. An effective diuretic, brooklime was formerly used in the treatment of gout and dropsy.

Burdock

Arctium lappa (Compositae)
Biennial or short-lived perennial
Beggar's buttons, gypsy's rhubarb

Native to northern Europe, the handsome burdock is known best from Victorian domestic beer-making as an ingredient of dandelion and burdock 'wine'. In Japan it is cultivated as a vegetable; the young stalks can be boiled and eaten hot or cold, or may even be candied. It is employed widely in folk medicine for treating skin problems and today is recognised to contain antibiotic properties. An infusion of leaves and root is thought to cleanse the blood or, used as a face rinse, will revitalise the skin. Grow burdock from spring-sown seed and the plants will flower the following season. Allow space in the herb border as burdock reaches as much as a metre in height and holds its leaves and flowerheads well, rather in the form of a Christmas tree. It would make an unusual dot plant in the herb garden. The burs themselves are deep reddish in colour and dry well for indoor decoration and children are always amused by the way they will adhere to clothing by their hooked spines. The first year root is the part used, with its slightly sweet scent and flavour not unlike that of licorice.

Button snakeroot

Liatris spicata (Compositae)   Perennial
Devil's bite, gay's feather, blazing star

Handsome upstanding flower spikes in August commend this medicinal species as a garden plant. The flowers are a rich crimson-purple and the leaves spatulate, but it is for the tuberous root that it is grown. Powdered root and leaves can be added to pot-pourri and sachets destined for wardrobes as it is considered to be an insect repellent. The flavour is bitter, hence its common name, and it can be employed as a gargle for sore throats. There are several white-flowered forms of particular decorative value in the herb garden as the plant blooms in late summer and into the autumn. 'Alba' is the most popularly cultivated cultivar but 'Floristan White' is worth seeking out although botanically both are *L. callilepsis* – much less worthy of inclusion in the herb border but, as white-flowered snakeroots, admissable for their interest. All *Liatris* require a moist soil and unlike many herbs respond to a spring mulch of leaf mould. Remember to water them during dry summers.

Camphor plant
Balsamita vulgaris (Compositae)   Perennial

This is not the camphor of commerce (that is *Cinamomum camphora*) but a herbaceous perennial bearing white, rather flimsy, daisy-like flowers in June and July. Given a dry sheltered position, with its striking leaves it will look well at the middle or back of the border. It has a tendency to lean on its neighbours, but twiggy pea sticks pushed in early in the season will support it adequately. The foliage alone merits its inclusion in any garden, for it is glaucous, grey-green, smooth, cool to the touch and highly aromatic of camphor when bruised. Add a leaf or two to pot-pourri because they retain their fragrance well on drying. When dried and crushed, the leaves will act as a moth deterrent for blanket cupboards.

Caraway
Carum carvi (Umbelliferae)   Biennial

Caraway, cultivated for its aromatic seed, is a good plant for a moderately heavy soil where there is some shade. The foliage is feathery and the young leaves have a mild parsley-like flavour, not at all like that of the seed. It can be chopped and added to soups and salads or used whole for garnishing. The flowers are tiny and white, appearing in July and August, and are followed by the familiar black seed. Once the seeds ripen, the heads need to be cut and the seeds allowed to fall naturally, when fully ripe, on to a sheet of paper. They are used for flavouring confectionery and liqueurs. Harvest the flower stalks and leave the plants until a week or two later. They can then be harvested for their carrot-like root, which may be used as a vegetable.

Catmint
Nepeta cataria (Labiatae)   Perennial
Catnep, catnip

The true medicinal catnep has whitish or pale mauve flowers from June to September and small downy foliage. Strictly it is a perennial but so short-lived that it invariably behaves as a biennial. On the whole it is an unassuming plant but useful for its mint-scented leaves, which can be used to make catnip tea. Before the introduction of tea this was a household beverage.

Closely associated, and planted in many herb gardens for its deep blue-grey overall effect, is catmint, *Nepeta* x *faassenii*. Less refined in flavour, the leaves do not have the clean crisp aroma of the true catnep. Both plants hold a fascination for cats and their attention can prevent plants from forming a good shape. There is an old garden saying about these plants:

> If you set it, cats will eat it,
> If you sow it, the cats don't know it.

Only when it has been bruised and the aroma released do cats take notice of it, so transplanted divisions attract most attention.

Centaury

Centaurium minus, Syn *Erythraea centaurium* (Gentianaceae)
Perennial, sometimes biennial

The little pink-flowered centaury, as a wild flower, varies in stature and appearance according to where it grows. So expect it to behave in the same way in the garden and probably vary in appearance from one garden to another. A dry soil produces a small spiky plant and rich soil a more abundant one. An emblem of good luck, it stands up well from a basal rosette of leaves and makes a good front of the border plant. Set it out in a group rather than stringing plants along the edge of the border. The bitter tasting quality of its leaves is said to stimulate the appetite and it is therefore widely incorporated in herbal tonics, digestive herbal teas and in liqueurs as a bitter herb.

Chamomile

Chamaemelum nobile (Compositae)   Perennial

Chamomile is a ragged, creamy-flowered little plant that sends out running shoots around itself. The double-flowered form is the one to cultivate in the herb garden, to provide dried flowerheads for chamomile tea. Four young fresh flowers or four to six dried ones can be infused to make a cupful of tea. The flowers should be gathered fresh before the petals turn brown at the back. 'Treneague' is

Chamomile.

the form to plant to make a chamomile lawn or bank, or the one to plant among paving stones, where it can be trodden upon to give off its sweet fragrance. It is a non-flowering form. The shoots quickly run about, forming a good mat-like growth of fruity fragrance, especially noticeable in warmer weather after a shower. Sandy loam provides the best medium for its roots and it likes good drainage and some sunshine.

A close relative, German chamomile (*Matricaria chamomilla*), is used in homeopathic medicine. In general appearance it is more weedy, with chalk-white single flowers with pronounced yellow centres.

Close-planted chamomile around a sundial at Hatfield House.

Chervil

Anthriscus cerefolium (Umbelliferae)   Annual

Chervil is cultivated chiefly for its pungent lacy foliage which strongly resembles the common cow parsley in appearance. At its best when young, the foliage is added to soups, sauces or egg dishes to impart its distinctive parsley-anise flavour. It is an ingredient of *fines herbes* and used habitually in French cooking, either dried or fresh, when it is chopped or used as a tasty garnish.

Sow a pinch of seed at regular intervals from spring to autumn to maintain a continuous supply of young leaves, because only these are used. Winter plants can be had by growing a plant or two in pots or boxes in a cool greenhouse. It seems to be rather particular about soil and likes a medium loam which is unlikely to dry out during the summer. Dappled shade suits it best.

Chicory

Cichorium intybus (Compositae)   Perennial
Succory

The exquisite china-blue daisy flowers of the chicory are studded along the stem but have only the briefest of lives. Fresh flowers appear daily and the plants remain in bloom from July to September. In chalky districts such as the Chilterns these blue flowers are a feature of the hedgerows. The foliage resembles that of the dandelion in shape and the young leaves may be chopped for use, but later they become unacceptably bitter in flavour. They can be blanched for salads by covering the plant crowns early in the year with rhubarb forcing pots or old buckets.

Horticultural varieties are grown because the wild plant

Chicory.

is exceedingly bitter in flavour, and the whole family is variable. Several are blanched. Most are of ancient cultivation for both culinary and medicinal use.

The ground root of Brunswick or Magdaberg chicory is used commercially as an adulterant in coffee.

Chives

Allium schoenoprasum (Liliaceae)   Perennial

Chives have hollow grass-like leaves and form clumps, making them particularly good as edging plants. The most refined member of the onion family, they provide a clean, sharp but mild flavour, and the dainty leaves when chopped make an excellent garnish. There is a larger form, usually known as giant chives, with a somewhat stronger flavour.

The true chives like sandy to medium loam but they tolerate chalk and like a spot where there is some shade in the course of the day. Sow seed in spring and use the fresh foliage throughout the season from April to September. No plant should be stripped of all its foliage unless it is to be discarded. Where good quality foliage is required, the rose pink or purple flowers should be prevented from blooming, but the herb garden is then deprived of one of its most attractive flowers. Use the little leaves to decorate salads or a platter of cheese or sandwiches, or float them in consommé.

Christmas rose

Helleborus niger (Ranunculaceae)   Perennial

Like many healing herbs taken in small measured doses, the Christmas rose is valued in both orthodox and homeopathic medicine, although it is poisonous, or at least highly toxic. A more pure and innocent-looking flower could not be found, braving the inclement weather in the winter garden. All parts of the plant are poisonous, as are the other hellebores native to Britain. They were all used by medieval herbalists as strong purgatives and local anaesthetics. The hellebore was one of the truly 'knockout' drugs that used to be soaked into a vinegar or wine sponge to administer to patients before major surgery such as the amputation of a limb.

In the garden it loves a moisture-retentive loam and, once established, likes to be left undisturbed. The dark green seven or nine fingered leaves make no great show during the summer, but in the winter the plant attracts a great deal of attention and it has increased in popularity as a decorative Christmas emblem.

Clary

Salvia sclarea (Labiatae)   Biennial
Clary sage, muscatel sage, clear eye

From spring-sown seed a drift of clary plants will flower the following year throughout the summer and into the autumn until the cold nights begin. They will seed themselves thereafter to inhabit the herb garden until weeded out. Strongly aromatic of muscatel – and in commerce the principal source of muscatel oil – the clary is a typical labiate with rough square stems and white, lavender or pink flowers. The vernacular name is a corruption of 'clear eye' and from the Latin *clarus* relating to the use of its seeds to rid the eyes of grit; when soaked in water they become mucilaginous. In herbal medicine it is included to treat vomiting and to lower a fever.

Coltsfoot

Tussilago farfara (Compositae)   Perennial
Coughwort, horsehoof

Coltsfoot is not a plant to introduce into the garden except in waste corners or where it can be strictly controlled by sinking an old dustbin or bucket to restrict the wandering roots. But in representative collections of medicinal plants it adds gay yellow flowers, with stems encased in purplish grey bracts, early in the year before most other plants come into flower. It is not encountered in hedge bottoms and on railway banks as often as it used to be. In bud the flowers are upturned, then hang their heads with a seemingly half-open flower, only to stand upright again as they fade. They like a dampish soil.

Felted leaves follow after the flowers have faded. They are rounded and deeply cordate at the base, on a furrowed stalk. They can be collected and dried for inclusion in herbal tobacco or burned along with the roots to relieve obstinate coughs.

Comfrey

Symphytum officinale (Boraginaceae)   Perennial
Knitbone, consound, boneset

A rough hairy plant, erect in habit, comfrey has drooping flowers, bell-like in little groups, blue, pink, cream or white. The leaves are rather unpleasant to handle, rough and clammy, but if collected before the plant flowers they may be used as a poultice or compress for sprains or to make an infusion to bathe painful joints. The pounded root forms a mucilaginous mass which hardens upon drying and was therefore used in the past to soak bandages to bind broken bones, acting as a plaster – hence the vernacular name of boneset.

A plant of dampish soils or waste ground and riverbanks, comfrey when cultivated needs soil that retains some moisture in summer in either half-shade or sunshine. Propagation is by division of roots in spring or autumn.

Two other species are cultivated: blue comfrey, *Symphytum caucasicum*, and Russian comfrey, *Symphytum peregrinum*. The latter seems to enjoy bursts of popularity as quickly maturing compost material for the organic gardening enthusiast and is a fodder plant. The blue or Caucasian comfrey is a smaller plant, with delightful deep blue flowers in April and May. Although it is a wanderer, it is useful for underplanting shrubs, provided the soil there is not too parched. Propagation is by division of the fleshy roots or from root cuttings taken in November.

Coriander

Coriandrum sativum (Umbelliferae)   Annual

The round beige seeds or fruits of coriander are familiarly recognised as a flavouring for pickles and curries. Their aroma is pleasant but before ripening the entire plant is distinctly odorous. Once the fragrance develops in August and September, the seed should be collected, or the whole plant harvested and dried so that the seed will fall naturally.

In the late twentieth century, through ethnic influences, European cuisine recognised the value of the aromatic leaves. They are widely added to salads and to both fish and vegetarian dishes, or used as a garnish. Sow the seed in spring, in almost any soil, in an open sunny situation along a shallow drill, thinning later. The whole plant is dainty in appearance, the lower leaves fan-like, the upper ones filigree, and the tiny flowers in July are mauve.

Corn salad

Valerianella olitoria (Valerianaceae)   Annual
Lamb's lettuce, white pot herb

Though strictly a biennial plant, corn salad comes to maturity so quickly that it is grown as an annual. It is perfectly hardy and makes a good salad plant for intercropping in summer although germination is often slow during warm weather. Cover the beds with newspaper and keep it wet to hasten the process. Apart from summer crops, a succession can be had by sowing in the autumn and overwintering under cloches for an early spring supply of soft green leaves and a richer crop. Gerard said of this little herb: 'We know the Lamb's Lettuce as Loblollie; and it serves in winter as a salad herb among others none the worst.' The flowers are minute, pale lilac green and insignificant, but it is advisable to use the plants before they appear. The younger the leaves, the more refined the flavour, although some people find it insipid.

Cotton lavender

see Lavender cotton

Cowslip

Primula veris (Primulaceae)   Perennial
Paigle, keys of heaven

All over western Europe there is a tradition that this plant sprang from the ground wherever St Peter dropped his keys – hence the English, French and German names, keys of heaven, *clef de St Pierre* and *schlüsselblumen*.

In early spring the sweetest and richest scent of all the herb flowers is provided by the heads of nodding golden yellow cowslip bells, each stem surrounded by a frilled rosette of leaves. Remember they are not to be dug up from the wild, so begin the collection from spring sown seed and once the colony is established the roots can be divided and replanted successfully in autumn. Herbal uses are becoming arcane; where once cowslip syrup may have been used in the treatment of bronchitis or even pneumonia it is now merely an ingredient of sedative teas or home-made wine. The flowers can be candied to decorate Easter confectionery.

Note: People allergic to primulas must avoid using cowslips as they can cause a skin rash.

Cumin

Cuminum cyminum (Umbelliferae)   Annual
Chinese parsley

The seed is the part used, when ground, for flavouring curries and pickles. It is a typical and habitual ingredient of Indian curries and many other eastern dishes.

Sow the seed in early April, to get a good start to the season's growth, for cumin matures slowly and the seed needs to be ripe by the middle of August. Sow in well drained soil in a sunny protected spot where the plant's lolling habit is not going to offend. The foliage is delicate, and the entire plant lacking in substance so that it sprawls about. Small flowers bloom in high summer – mauve, pink and white – followed by round seeds. When chopped as flavouring or garnish, the foliage earns the name of Chinese parsley, for it is a typical ingredient of Chinese cooking.

Curry plant

Helichrysum serotinum (Compositae)   Perennial

A curry-like aroma pervades the air around this sub-shrub, especially strong in warm moist weather. In the aromatic garden it can be excessive and can easily

overpower a sweeter or more delicate fragrance. As a garden plant its chief attribute is the tinsel-like silver-white foliage, which sparkles, especially after a shower of rain.

Its strong aroma perhaps suggests its use as a flavouring, but it should not be used in this way. (It has been known to cause vomiting.) It is generally considered to be doubtfully hardy in many districts and its real value as a garden plant is its decorative appearance. In winter the foliage is less

Curry plant.

silver and rather more turquoise grey. Rusty metallic yellow flowers appear in June and July. Propagation is from summer cuttings.

Dandelion

Taraxacum officinale (Compositae)   Perennial

The much abused dandelion, which if it were a rare plant would probably be a prized garden treasure, needs no description. Flower stalks need to be removed if the leaves are cultivated as salad, and the early young leaves are less bitter and far superior in texture for eating fresh. Leaves can be blanched early in the year by covering the crowns with upturned flower pots, plastic buckets or black polythene hoods. The winter foliage can be cooked like spinach and seems to be preferable when mixed with sorrel, though it then forms a strong diuretic. Crowns can be lifted and forced during the winter to produce soft green succulent growth. Some continental named varieties are occasionally available.

The flat tufted yellow flowers, always so prolific in the wild, make a good wine, and the leaves and roots are used to lend a bitterness to herb beers.

The roots are ground and used as a caffeine-free coffee, and they are often considered to be a sedative. Lift the roots at the end of the season, scrub and dry, before grinding for coffee.

Dill

Anethum graveolens (Umbelliferae)   Annual

Dill water was a remedy for restive infants in the early part of the twentieth century and dill is still the sweet tasting content of the proprietary gripe water.

In the kitchen its main use is in dill vinegar, which is made by macerating half a cup of dill seed in a litre of malt vinegar for three or four hours, then straining off the liquor for storage. In pickled cucumbers, a sprig of the whole plant with half-ripe seed is often an ingredient and gives a soured flavour.

Sow the seed in shallow drills in March or April, in a well drained soil and sunny position, thinning later. The filmy foliage may be collected from about six to eight weeks after sowing, to flavour fish dishes or to sprinkle on potatoes as is habitual in Poland and the Czech Republic.

The flavour is lighter than that of the seed, so sprigs of foliage are always added fresh after cooking.

The tiny yellow flowers in July and August add little to the appearance of the herb garden but then, as the round seeds form, the whole flowerheads make an effective display.

Elder

Sambucus nigra (Caprifoliaceae)   Shrub
Elderberry

Elder grows easily from cuttings and is a rampant grower, feeding grossly and demanding light and space wherever it is introduced. For garden effect choose the golden-leaved form 'Aurea', whose foliage deepens as the season progresses, or, better still for decorative effect, *Sambucus racemosa* 'Plumosa Aurea' – the red-berried elder. This form has beautifully slashed golden leaves and creamy yellow flowerheads and is far more garden-worthy than *Sambucus nigra*.

The berries of both are edible and are used popularly for winemaking or they can be dried and added to confectionery like small currants. When the luscious black berries of the common elder are sprinkled into stewed apple as it cooks or added to apple pie, they lend an attractive pink colour. Alternatively, when the flowers are added to cooked apple, pear or gooseberry, they impart a muscatel flavour. Do not eat the berries raw, for their purgative effect is fierce, but when cooked they are more acceptable and can be added to jams, jellies and syrups. Fresh berries can be stored in the freezer.

Countless old recipes exist, suggesting delightful uses to which the plant can be put. Elderflower fritters, using a light batter, sprinkled with sugar make a delicious and unusual dessert. An old recipe for 'sambocade' uses elderflowers combined with curd cheese and egg white in a tart. Elderflower tea has a tranquillising action and soothes headaches and throat infections, although it is the berries that are mainly employed medicinally in the treatment of sore throats and coughs. Hot elderberry juice is a good household remedy for colds and influenza.

One of the best cosmetic herbs, elderflowers have for centuries been used to cure sunburn and remove freckles and coax wrinkles away. Elderflower water is an excellent skin cleanser.

Elecampane.

Elecampane

Inula helenium (Compositae)   Perennial
Scabwort, horseheal, velvet dock

A large handsome perennial, elecampane revels in moisture-retentive, good rich soil, where a stout clump can form. Bright yellow, rather shaggy daisy-like flowers bloom in midsummer, the petals becoming rather spiky and floppy as the flower matures. Grown for its aromatic root since Roman times, it is a good plant to introduce into the decorative herb garden because the clumps form well and establish quickly and it towers above most of the gentler herbs.

A pungent oil renders the roots astringent and strongly antiseptic, so that it has been used both for infected throats as candied lozenges and as an aid to digestion. Formerly the lozenges were coloured with cochineal and sold as a sweetmeat considered to be a treatment for bronchial and asthmatic attacks.

The vernacular names scabwort and horseheal denote its use as a veterinary treatment for the skin eruptions of farm animals. A strong diffusion of the leaves or a decoction of the root is needed, and it has been reported as being efficacious in cases of acne in adolescents.

Propagation is by division of a root clump in autumn, or by spring-sown seed. If the foliage is to be used it is best gathered young, but, to be valuable, the roots must be left to mature fully before being lifted at the end of the season, after the flowers have faded.

Evening primrose

Oenothera biennis (Onagraceae)   Biennial
Evening star, tree primrose

The evening primrose grows in dry waste places and in the garden likes best a well drained light position, although it is not too selective of soil. Its main attribute is the sweet perfume in the evenings from the flimsy pale yellow flowers. The flowering period is long, extending throughout June, July and August and often into September. As the season progresses the flowers seem to stay open more during the day, but their evening habit of advertising their presence is to attract the insects that are on the wing during the twilight hours, for pollination.

A strong tap root is formed quickly, so care needs to be taken even when transplanting seedlings. During the second season the leaves and the bark of the stem are effective in the treatment of gastro-intestinal disorders, and there are reports of success in the treatment of whooping cough. Harvest and dry the whole plant in the summer of the second year. The mature root may be used as a vegetable like parsnip, and scientists are investigating it as a possible cure for multiple sclerosis, and other degenerative diseases.

Considerable progress has been made in researching the finer properties of the evening primrose. The seed contains a rare oily acid which is proving invaluable in reducing premenstrual tension and a number of menopausal symptoms. Further, there appears to be substantial evidence that it reduces the incidence of thrombosis.

Fennel

Foeniculum vulgare (Umbelliferae)   Perennial

A tall growing, superbly graceful plant, ideal for the back of the herb border, fennel is easily recognised by its long finely cut soft foliage. The stems are firmly upstanding and the foliage showers around it, topped by small yellow flowers from July to September. A bronze-leaved variety, often sold as black fennel, is very attractive.

Fennel.

Leaves and stems can be picked fresh throughout the summer and impart an anise-like flavour to salads or fish dishes. The foliage does not dry well, but the young shoots may be dried and stored for winter flavouring. The seed is aromatic, slightly bitter, with a less sweet anise flavour than the foliage, and is used to garnish bread and cakes. Where the flavour is enjoyed, there is a variety of ways in which it can be introduced: chopped foliage in salads or yoghurt, for example. Or, simply by baking bread on a bed of fennel stalks, a subtlety of flavour is imparted.

Sow the seed at stations along a drill in April and thin out subsequently to about 50 cm apart to allow the plants to spread. Alternatively, sow *in situ* in the border to form groups, allowing a reasonable distance between plants.

An annual fennel, grown for its bulbous stem-leaf base, is Florence fennel or finnochio (*Foeniculum vulgare* var *dulce*, sometimes listed as *Foeniculum dulce*). Used as a vegetable, served with a white or cheese sauce, it is delicious. Seed ought not to be sown until the soil has warmed up well, or it can be started indoors or under glass and the seedlings planted out later. It is the bulbous base that is eaten late in the summer or early autumn, and it does well only in warm summers.

Fenugreek

Trigonella foenum-graecum (Leguminosae)   Annual
Greek hayseed

A tender plant from the Mediterranean regions, fenugreek is now increasingly cultivated in gardens, but is only successful in warm summers. Typical of its family, the pea flowers are creamy white and the leaves trifoliate, soft and with a sheen.

It is known best as a spicy ingredient of curry powder or when roasted as a coffee substitute. The flavour is warm and pungent. The name 'Greek hayseed' alludes to its cultivation as a fodder plant and as a scented constituent of inferior or damaged hay mixtures. The seed adds a flavour to the foliage which cattle are said to like. It is a common ingredient of veterinary conditioning powders. The seed is aromatic and can be eaten when sprouted as a tasty salad ingredient, the flavour emanating from the seeds themselves. The soaked seed takes on a maple syrup flavour, which enhances confectionery.

Feverfew

Tanacetum parthenium, Syn *Chrysanthemum parthenium*
(Compositae)   Perennial
Featherfew, featherfoil

Feverfew is an old cottage garden plant, naturalised in many localities, and at its best where it has seeded itself. It will select gravel drive edges, old walls or roughly paved areas and will lend an air of informality to the site. Introduce it into any dry sunny corner of the garden by seed sown in spring or autumn, or by root division, or even from summer cuttings. It makes a pretty edging to beds and is an attractive plant to use to outline flower beds or beds in the general herb garden. Strictly it is a perennial, though rather short-lived, but it seeds itself so freely that it is ever present.

Its aromatic yellowish green leaves are strongly reminiscent of those of the chrysanthemum. It has ribbed stems and a profusion of small daisy-like white flowers with yellow centres, from midsummer onwards. The dried

foliage acts as a moth deterrent or, when used fresh, relieves insect bites. Renewed interest in feverfew has centred upon its use in the reduction of mild muscle spasms and of migraine. Several new healing substances containing extracts from feverfew have been patented and it is estimated that about 70 per cent of migraine sufferers report some relief from the use of this plant. A few leaves in a bread sandwich as part of a daily diet is, in itself, said to be helpful to sufferers.

Feverfew.

Foxglove

Digitalis purpurea (Scrophulariaceae)   Biennial
Fairy thimbles

The drug digitalis is obtained from the soft green leaves of the common foxglove and, although much is imported today, one or two of the larger manufacturing chemists have their own digitalis farms in England. The plant is poisonous.

Foxgloves are a must for the decorative herb garden or representative collection of medicinal plants. The common

Foxglove.

purple foxglove likes cool shade and while it is quite happy on light soils it needs a cool root run with some compost or moisture-retentive material incorporated. Self-sown seedlings thrive best and, while they are true biennial plants, a late formed rosette may persist for the whole of the second year and flower only the following season. They should be propagated from seed sown in May or June where they are expected to flower. Plant them at the middle to the back of the border or scatter in dappled shade beneath overhanging trees.

Often their spire form is better appreciated when they can be seen against a green or darkened background. The foliage is tongue-shaped, dark green, deeply veined and soft, but the plant's beauty lies in the one-sided flower spire with dangling purplish red bells, spotted within. These have earned several descriptive country names for the plant: fairy cap, fairy glove, lady's thimble, witch's thimble, dead man's bellows, dragon's mouth or, simply, cottagers – because they belong to the poor people.

Garlic

Allium sativum (Liliaceae)   Perennial

Garlic is often associated with highly flavoured cooked meats, and the aroma is far too strong and sulphurous for some palates. But it is used increasingly in sophisticated culinary practices, adding a subtlety of flavour which no other plant imparts. Medicinally, its use is cleansing to the blood and it is of benefit to many catarrh sufferers.

Garlic offsets need to be planted in September to allow them to establish before the winter, for the best results; or a start can be made as soon as possible in February or March so that a long growing season can be allowed, but so often a cold or wet spring leads to poor crops of garlic. Break up the bulb into individual cloves, and handle them carefully to avoid bruising. Push them upright into the soil just below the surface. They need to be planted in short rows or planted in a block over a small area. Prevent the white flowers from blooming by nipping them out, so that the bulbs will mature in summer. The top growth will begin to turn colour when they are ripe.

A small quantity of garlic added to meat dishes, stews or cooked meats will heighten any existing flavour, and a fresh broken clove rubbed round a salad bowl will improve any green salad enormously. If too much is eaten, so that the aroma hangs on the breath, relieve it by chewing parsley.

Gentian

Gentiana lutea (Gentianaceae)   Perennial
Bitterwort

The yellow gentian was the first of its genus to be introduced into cultivation in Britain, and the herbalist John Gerard (1545–1612) grew it in his garden, calling it felwort. Gentian bitters are extracted from the enormous spongy root, which plunges down into the soil as much as a metre. In the Alps, where its statuesque growth is a feature of low meadow slopes, the roots are lifted in autumn, when they are richest in gentianin, and made into gentian brandy. The bitterness of the root makes it one of the most effective tonics.

As a garden plant, in a representative medicinal collection, it takes a while to establish itself but can live for a couple of generations where it is happy. The yellow star-like flowers are clustered around the stem at intervals, in July and August, held by important-looking cup-shaped leaves, which in parts enfold the flowers. Propagation is by seed, but the seedlings need to be transplanted with care, so that the brittle young roots are not damaged.

Germander

Teucrium chamaedrys (Labiateae)   Perennial
Wall germander

Formerly much cultivated for its medicinal properties, germander's claim to inclusion in the herb garden nowadays is as a substantial edging plant. It is one of the aromatic plants that was used to outline the Tudor knot garden and can be clipped to retain a formal shape.

Its principal use was in the treatment of flatulence, to aid digestion and as a flavouring for liqueurs and tonic wines. It imparts a bitter clean flavour.

The small dark green leaves are shaped like those of the oak. Tiny rosy flowers appear in June and July, but the foliage is the main attribute.

Propagated by seed sown in the spring or from summer cuttings, it soon forms a good bushy little plant which is perfectly hardy in spite of its southern European origins. Almost any soil supports it, and it is tolerant of some light shade.

Goat's rue

Galega officinalis (Leguminosae)   Perennial

This pretty, light-hearted plant always adds a decorative touch to the herb garden. The foliage is soft and typical of the family and the flowers are carried in short spikes of sweet-pea shaped blooms of mauve and blue (sometimes white) in June and July. Its rather untidy habit suggests that it ought to be put at the back of the border where it can be concealed after flowering. Good twiggy pea sticks provide suitable stakes, which it will obliterate as the season proceeds.

It is from the dried flowering shoots that a tisane is made for diabetes, especially of the elderly. Ancient lore credits it as a stimulant to lactation and as a plant fed to animals for this purpose. Modern herbals seem to regard this action as doubtful, but it is an allusion to this property that has given it its common name of goat's rue, the foliage being not dissimilar to that of rue.

Good King Henry

Chenopodium bonus henricus (Chenopodiaceae) Perennial
Goosefoot, mercury, allgood

In much the same way that spinach is used today, Good

Good King Henry.

King Henry was formerly used as a vegetable. Its renewed appearance in the kitchen garden is apparent, and the soft arrow-shaped leaves, when boiled and flavoured with a sprinkling of lemon juice, make a good green-leaf vegetable. The green young shoots may be peeled, boiled and used in the same way as asparagus. It is considered to be a highly nutritious vegetable.

Cultivate it on well worked loamy soil and it will continue to produce for a number of years. Sow seed in drills in April, thinning subsequently, and allow the plants to establish themselves during the first year, cutting only in subsequent years. Always leave enough foliage on the plant to maintain it in health. Established plants can be divided in April.

The vernacular name smearwort refers to its use as an ingredient of an ointment to cleanse chronic skin eruptions.

Ground ivy

Glechoma hederacea (Labiatae)　　　　　　　Perennial
Alehoof, gill-over-the-ground

This is a common wild flower of northern Europe including Britain, where it is cleared away as a weed in many gardens. (Often, other gardeners think herb growers are crazy to cultivate weeds!) Pieces of the long runners that straggle over the ground, if planted in the herb border, will establish themselves quickly because tiny roots burst forth at almost every node (leaf joint). Purple pink flowers, somewhat bugle-shaped, nestle around the square stem at every joint, and there are pretty rounded leaves with pinked cut edges and glands that contain an aromatic oil. It is these oils that have gained the name alehoof for the ancient herb as it was used to clear and flavour ale before the introduction of hops.

A tea, known as gill tea, was a popular country spring tonic and remedy for colds, kidney complaints and to comfort the low abdominal aches of menstruation, especially for young girls.

Henbane

Hyoscyamus niger (Solanaceae)　　　　Annual or biennial
Henbell, belene

In appearance the henbane seems to be an evil plant, and it was one of those that used to be closely associated with madness and delirium, part of the witches' brew, full of magical powers and highly poisonous. It is little wonder that in unskilled hands it had drastic effects. To add to the mysterious air, both annual and biennial seedlings can come from seed from the same capsule. Its slightly foetid smell, coming from the pale, prickly and somewhat sticky leaves, does not endear it. The flowers appear to be mauve but are really cream, so thickly pencilled with purple lines that only on close inspection is their beauty seen. The green-brown seed capsules late in the season resemble decayed human teeth and under the doctrine of signatures were interpreted as signifying that the plant should be used in the relief of toothache. This is the plant, used in extract, that Dr Crippen employed in murdering his wife.

Horehound

Marrubium vulgare (Labiatae)   Perennial
Hoarhound

The white horehound, so called because the silky hairs that adorn the plant give it a frosty appearance, has a

Horehound.

strong smell and the extract of the leaves is extremely bitter in flavour. The leaves are much wrinkled and dusty or hairy in appearance, and the stems also are felted with hairs. A candy is made for the alleviation of coughs by boiling down the washed herbs until the juice is extracted or by using an electrical juice extractor and boiling the resultant liquid with sugar until it is thick enough to set when cooled. The quantities necessary are at least 750 grams of sugar to a litre of liquid. Gather the herb just before flowering for it to be most effective.

A hardy native plant, not much seen growing in the wild these days, it needs a drying, poor soil to flourish in the garden. Propagation is by division in spring and often it does not flower the summer after being divided.

The offensive smell of black horehound (*Ballota nigra*) keeps it from being much cultivated. It has rose-purple flowers and less hairy leaves than the white horehound.

Horseradish

Armoracia rusticana (Cruciferae)   Perennial

A coarse-growing perennial whose natural home is eastern Europe, horseradish is grown for its tapering fleshy root, which provides the condiment. The taste is biting,

Horseradish.

mustard-like and very penetrating, only at its best when the root has been grated or thinly sliced. When it is unbroken it is inodorous and so can be stored easily for quite a long period. Formerly it was used as a cosmetic, considered to be effective in clearing freckles and maintaining a clear complexion. It is also used in the same way as a mustard plaster, to give relief to aching joints.

On account of its deeply thrusting root, the horseradish requires a deeply worked soil and is usually raised from root cuttings or pieces of root planted out in February or March. Some roots can be left in the ground at the end of the growing season to provide pieces for the following spring. Others can be stored and used for the kitchen. Renew the bed of horseradish about every third year.

Hound's tongue

Cynoglossum officinale (Boraginaceae)   Perennial
Gipsyflower, scaldhead, rosenoble

Hound's tongue is a stout plant, tough of texture, with leaves resembling the shape and roughness of a dog's tongue. The herbalist Gerard said also: 'It will tye the tongues of Houndes so that they shall not bark at you, if it be laid under the bottom of your feet.' Previous to Gerard, it had been administered in the belief that it could cure stuttering. When the doctrine of signatures was a prevalent belief, this resemblance led to the use of the plant in the treatment of dog bite.

Although it is a British native plant it is not commonly found in the wild state. But seed is available and as a garden plant it thrives best on gravel or sandy soil and it tolerates both drought and exposure without ill effects, making a suitable plant for a seaside herb garden. The little bur-like seeds are covered with tiny hooked spines and ought to be sown in August.

The name scaldhead is a combination of two uses to which an impregnated grease or oil of hound's tongue was formerly put: firstly as an application to scalds, and secondly to rub over a bald head in the firm belief that hair would be restored.

Houseleek

Sempervivum tectorum (Crassulaceae)   Perennial
Thunder plant, Jupiter's beard, jubarb

Houseleek.

The bareness of its habitat and its undemanding nature make the houseleek an easy plant to cultivate. Sometimes it can appear slow to establish. Planting the tiny offsets at almost any time of the year between paving stones or in crannies or around the edges of a trough – anywhere where a porous environment encourages the roots to form – is sufficient to start a colony. The conglomerate growth is always cool to the touch: each wedge-shaped leaf is a living reservoir, enabling the plant to survive in seemingly adverse conditions.

Herbalists regard it as one of the safest remedies for inflammation and swelling, and a portion of bruised leaf is recommended to be rubbed over the affected part. A fresh leaf crushed above the eye so as to exude the juice directly in was reputed to dispel styes and clear inflammation but it is always important to seek advice before self-treatment for the eyes.

The English name of thunder plant is reminiscent of a belief, widespread in Europe in the Dark Ages, that to have houseleek growing on a roof was a charm against being struck by lightning. More practically, the name *Sempervivum tectorum* means 'ever living plant of the roof' and suggests that it was mainly established there to retain the roofing material.

Hyssop.

Hyssop

Hyssopus officinalis (Labiatae)   Perennial

An aromatic shrubby little evergreen with tiny blue flowers from June to September and small leaves, hyssop is attractively employed as an edging plant in the herb garden. It is often overlooked: its appearance is unassuming but its aroma is pungent and distinctive. The foliage needs to be rubbed to release it, but fresh leaves sprinkled into soups and stews add piquancy.

Both flowers and leaves dry well and are good ingredients for pot-pourri as they retain their aroma. If the flowers are gathered as they reach maturity and dried, they can be used to make an infusion which, together with honey, relieves chest troubles. If the fresh green growing tips are picked and dried in summer an infusion made from them is useful in the treatment of catarrh.

Propagation is from spring-sown seed or from summer cuttings taken with a heel. Hyssop prefers a light garden soil and sunny position. Once established, the plants tolerate clipping and so may be used as a formal edging. When they are to be used in this way the clippings ought to be preserved and dried as a harvest, as the plants will not tolerate a clipping *and* a harvesting.

Indian physic

Gillenia trifoliata (Rosaceae)   Perennial
Bowman's root, gillenia

As a perennial herb indigenous to the United States, where the American Indians and early colonists used the roots, Indian physic is an interesting plant to include in a collection of medicinal herbs. Its action is drastic (and perhaps suspect) but the root also provides a red dye.

It has oval veined leaves and dainty white flowers held well above them. The noteworthy characteristic of the plant is the red colouring of the stems and large calyces. It enjoys dappled shade in a slightly rich, moist loam.

Ivy

Hedera helix (Araliaceae)   Woody perennial

Ivy is poisonous in all parts of the plant and has never been accepted as a herb although many legends, suggestive of benevolent powers, surround it. It flowers in November

Ivy.

when nothing else in the herb garden has much life, so its main value there rests in the decorative-leaved forms. The smaller-leaved ivies, especially, will look dainty trailing over walls, around seats or covering old stumps or ornaments.

Once considered as effective against whooping cough, it was at the same time asserted that the patient would be able to see witches! The cosmetics industry has conducted wide research into plant products and ivy is now incorporated in some soothing 'after sun' creams that relieve the burning of the skin. It is suggested that it can reduce blistering and eliminate cellulite and is an ingredient of some modern cellulite creams.

Jacob's ladder

Polemonium caeruleum (Polemoniaceae)   Perennial
Greek valerian, charity

The common name refers to the shape of the little leaves: it is not a valerian, but there is a slight resemblance in the leaves and cats give their attention to this plant, as they do to valerian. As late as the mid nineteenth century it was used mainly as an anti-syphilitic agent and in the treatment of rabies. It has fallen out of use medicinally but appears to be being reintroduced into medicinal herb collections.

The helmet-shaped flowers are of an intense blue in midsummer, and there is a white-flowered form. A variegated-leaved form is also recorded. Propagation is from division of the creeping rootstock in spring or autumn, but the plants seed themselves so easily that there is usually a plentiful supply of young plants. They like any good garden soil, provided that there is no surface moisture.

Juniper

Juniperus communis (Coniferae)   Perennial

The ripe berries of the common juniper vary considerably in flavour according to where the shrubs grow, and it is apparent that some good sun baking is necessary to heighten and refine the flavour. Berries ought to be blue and sweet and resinous. Their flavour goes well in marinades, for rich meats such as venison and pork, and they are used in the making of sauerkraut. They need to be crushed in a mortar to release the full flavour. They are known best, perhaps, as a flavouring for gin and steinhager, when oil of juniper is usually used.

The shrub is difficult to buy, and there appears to be a dearth in garden centres and nurseries. But it can, with patience, be propagated from cuttings or from seed, which takes a long time to germinate. It is best to sow it in a seed pan and forget about it.

Lavender

Lavandula angustifolia (Labiatae)   Perennial

Lavender, the most readily recognised herb, can be included on two counts: for its decorative usefulness as a garden plant, and for its use in perfumery. The essential oil when extracted is known as oil of lavender and the quality depends as much upon climate as on the strain of the plant. Oil produced in England is some of the finest in the world, certainly richer than that produced in Mediterranean regions. Commercially lavender is grown for its oil, which is strongly antiseptic and which enjoys

Lavender.

popularity with the development of aromatherapy. The diluted oil can be used for cleaning wounds or relieving stings and can be rubbed on to aching joints and stiff limbs. For centuries it has been known as a cure for headaches and the Tudor botanist William Turner advocated that lavender flowers be woven into the hat to prevent headaches.

The gardener may well feel bewildered by the numerous kinds of lavender available, and yet they are an invaluable ingredient of the herb garden – and indeed of any flower garden. Basically, the flowers are mauve, borne in closely packed spikes which protrude on long stiff stems from the grey-leaved bush, like hat pins from a pincushion. John Gerard described them thus: 'the floures grow at the top of the branches, spike fashion, of a blew colour.'

The height varies from 15 to 60 cm according to the type, the smaller ones lending themselves to cultivation in containers or even for rock gardens. Large kinds form decorative internal hedges or edging to driveways and always look well in the herb garden.

Basically two main types are grown popularly, although the enthusiast will soon seek out some of the more unusual ones.

Lavandula angustifolia, flowering in June and July, forms a dome-shaped cushion with narrow downy leaves. The later flowering *L x intermedia* (also listed as lavandin) comes into flower in early August, lasting well into September in all but the wettest of seasons.

Cultivars of *L. angustifolia* are 'Folgate' with deliciously scented purple flowers; 'Royal Purple' and 'Imperial Gem', both tall with deep purple flowers that dry well; while 'Munstead' and 'Hidcote' (slow growing) are two more familiar ones. Of those bearing pink flowers, 'Miss Katherine', from Norfolk Lavender Farms, is good and tall, reaching perhaps 60-70 cm, with deep, long lasting flowers. 'Rosea' is familiar in herb gardens, smaller in stature and paler in flower colour, but nevertheless an old favourite.

Some attractive cultivars of *L x intermedia* include 'Twickel Purple', a plant well-known for its fulsome flower spikes of deep blue-purple; 'Grappenhall', another strong-growing plant sometimes reaching a metre in height; and 'Seal', excellent for drying, with richly fragrant, dark purple flowers in long heads. The so-called Dutch

Lavender at the Norfolk Lavender Centre.

lavenders, with blue-mauve flowers, have been grown in gardens for many years whereas 'Grosso', a cultivar grown commercially, is comparatively new.

A favourite, if not a familiar curiosity, is *L. stoechas*, the misnamed French lavender, sometimes also listed as Spanish lavender. A dense busy plant, rather more green than many other lavenders, it produces dark bright plum-purple flowers with a couple of 'wings' terminating the flower spike. Some authorities consider it to be a sub-species, *pedunculata*, and market it as 'Papillon' – alluding to its two wings that look as if a butterfly is visiting the flower.

Lavender has been grown commercially for a couple of hundred years in various parts of England for the richly scented oil it yields. English lavender or common lavender was the *L. angustifolia* type, while French-grown plants were *L. dentata*, today usually called either 'fringed lavender', because the edges of the grey-green leaves are toothed or fringed, or 'French lavender'. The scent is a little more camphorous than that of *angustifolia*. It is one of the less hardy lavenders and appreciates being grown in a container that can be brought into the conservatory for the winter and kept dry. Another half-hardy one is *L. viridis*, a curious plant with washed-out white flowers with green bracts. The flattish green leaves are aromatic of lemon and lavender.

Cultivars to select are: low growing (up to 45-50 cm) – 'Folgate', 'Munstead', 'Nama Alba', 'Hidcote', 'Hidcote Pink', 'Rosea', 'Lodden Blue'; medium growing (spreading to 30 cm, up to 60 cm) – 'Imperial Gem', 'Twickel Purple', 'Bowles Early'; tall growing (up to 70 cm) – 'Grappenhall', 'Seal', 'Grosso', 'Royal Purple', 'Miss Katherine'.

All lavenders prefer well-drained soil with a lime content and like to be firmly planted. Where lavender is grown for garden effect it is advisable to take a batch of cuttings each year to maintain a regular supply of young plants for replacements. The useful decorative effect of many lavender plants diminishes after five or six years and time spent on trying to refurbish them is better spent in grubbing them up and replacing with young plants. A leggy bush, bare at the base, is ugly and frequently tends to lean to one side. Propagation is from heeled cuttings taken in August and early September and rooted in sandy compost or a proprietary cutting compost.

The immense popularity of lavender in both the herb garden and the flower garden is out of proportion to its usefulness. Commercially, it is widely cultivated for its oil. It is grown domestically for its dryish flower spikes, useful for decoration and sweet-smelling conceits such as lavender bags. The foliage, as well as the flowers, is a good ingredient of pot-pourri.

Lavender bags. Both flowers and leaves can be used in pot-pourri and because the flowers hold their perfume so well on drying they are put into sachets. For this, the flower spikes are cut while in fat bud, before the petals unfurl, and are dried by spreading out the stems on paper or cloth in a warm room, garden shed or airing cupboard. Sunshine will bleach the colour, so shade the flowers while they are drying, and once the buds can be rubbed free of the stems they are ready for use. In a warm room this will take three to four weeks, less in a warm cupboard. Lavender is a powerful sternutatory, so a smog mask or even a simple respirator needs to be worn when rubbing the flowers – and protect domestic animals from the dust. The rubbed-off flowers are sieved to separate them from dust and bracts and are then ready for packing into sachets or small bags.

Lavender cotton

Santolina species (Compositae)   Perennial
Santolina, cotton lavender

Given full sun in a well-drained spot, the santolinas are among the best sub-shrubs with aromatic foliage. They are grown mainly for the grey-white foliage, which persists throughout the year, and benefit from being close-clipped in spring to encourage new growth and to prevent them from becoming leggy and developing bare patches in the centre. Propagation is by cuttings taken in the summer. *Santolina chamaecyparissus* (Syn *Santolina incana*) has thread-like foliage, resembling silver coral, and forms a cushion of growth which is decorated in July and August with yellow bobble flowers. The foliage is pungent and aromatic. The form *Santolina chamaecyparissus insularis*, catalogued sometimes as *Santolina neopolitana*, is slightly taller, softer and looser of habit, with feathered pungent foliage and, catalogued as 'Sulphurea', has primrose yellow flowers set off by rather greener leaves. It is a useful plant in the decorative herb garden. Another good species to try is *Santolina virens*, with compact bushy growth of emerald green, slightly oily to the touch and highly aromatic, almost camphorous.

Lavender cotton foliage, dried well, retains its aroma and is a good insecticide to scatter in cupboards and drawers, if the smell of camphor is liked. Combine some foliage with cloves in china pomanders for the wardrobe.

Lemon balm

Melissa officinalis (Labiatae)   Perennial
Sweet balm, balm

A rounded bush-like perennial with richly aromatic bright green leaves and somewhat insignificant flowers from mid to late summer, lemon balm is a true cottage garden plant and best in that form. A variegated-leaved form *M.o.* 'Variegata' is popularly cultivated but can appear somewhat messy. There is a golden-leaved form *M.o.* 'Aurea', worth growing in dappled shade to maintain the fresh butter-yellow colour. The rounded leaves are deeply veined, strongly scented of lemon with a rather stale overtone, so it is important to use them when they are young before the flowering period. The leaves dry well and may be included in pot-pourri.

Lemon balm.

A tea or tisane made from the fresh or dried leaves is delicious, flavoured with a little honey. It is a favourite herb tea, recommended particularly for fevers and colds to promote perspiration and 'bring the fever out'. The leaves may also be added to salads with some restraint and used dried in stuffings. Commercially they are employed in perfumery and in flavouring liqueurs.

Give lemon balm a good garden soil, retentive of moisture, in a sunny corner, or somewhere where it at least has some neighbours, for all true cottage garden plants like a friendly environment. Propagation is best carried out by division of roots in spring or autumn.

Lemon verbena

Lippia citriodora, Syn *Aloysia triphylla*, *Lippia triphylla* (Verbenaceae)   Perennial

A tender perennial which dies down each winter and is not suitable for cultivation out of doors in elevated or cool areas, lemon verbena is also a good plant for a conservatory or garden room and may be cultivated in a pot. Its long narrow pointed leaves have the purest and most refreshing aroma of all lemon-scented plants. The flower spikes are a secondary feature of the plant.

Out of doors, tuck it into a dry and very sheltered corner, at the base of a wall where the soil is none too good, then the roots will come through most winters. Use a leaf or two in pot-pourri – too much can unbalance the resultant mixture with a lemony sharpness, so definite is the scent. As with any other aromatic plant, the foliage is at its best just before the plant comes into bloom. A tisane can be made from the dried foliage, said to help snuffly noses.

Licorice

Glycyrrhiza glabra (Leguminosae)   Perennial

Although a familiar herb in the ancient world, licorice was introduced into cultivation in the western world in medieval times. John of Gaddesden (*c.*1280–1361) wrote of snails and licorice being the last ditch remedy for scrofulous glands and William Turner mentioned it in 1548 as being known to the apothecaries and in their physic gardens. But it was in the eighteenth century that the Dominican friars introduced it as a commercial crop to the Pontefract district of Yorkshire. When the manufacture of 'spanish' or Spanish licorice was in full progress, Pontefract cakes, stamped with the image of the town castle, were a popular item of confectionery.

It is the tap root which subdivides to produce great subsidiary roots up to 1.5 metres long that are used to make the sweet extract, invaluable as a medical flavouring or sweetening agent safe for diabetics, and trusted as a digestive, and as an ingredient of tobacco and snuff. It is understood to be still employed in the flavouring of Guinness.

In habit the plant resembles an ash seedling, and droops each evening. It is pale green, forming a bushy plant up to a metre in height. Tiny insignificant mauve-white flowers grow in the leaf axils in high summer.

Propagation is from root cuttings in spring, and as the plants become established it is usual to cut back the top growth to stimulate root formation. After three or four years, cutting back each year, the roots are harvested. Seed may also be sown in spring, or plants can be divided in spring or autumn.

Lily-of-the-valley

Convallaria majalis (Liliaceae)   Perennial
May lily

This is a poisonous plant, but one used in the treatment of cardiac conditions in eastern Europe. It should be grown in a herb garden only as a representative plant. Its twin broad leaves appear early in spring, spearing the ground in little rolls, and unfurl to enfold a single stem of pendulous, highly fragrant white bells.

Given a dampish woodland calcareous soil, the plants will quickly form a good colony, spreading by the stoloniferous roots. Propagation is by division of clumps or by breaking off a portion from the outside of the cluster of root mass.

Cultivation in pots is straightforward; lily-of-the-valley will scent a conservatory at Easter, and by careful management plants may be had in flower until June. Plump crowns are potted up in a Number 1 potting compost and leaf mould in the autumn and kept out of doors to settle. Once indoors keep them in a dark cool place until growth is about 13 cm in height. Admit light and give warmth gradually until they are taken into a warm living room and watered as growth proceeds. Specially retarded crowns can be purchased for forcing in this way. If planted out in the garden after flowering they may not flower the next year, but subsequently they will recover.

Many beds of lily-of-the-valley draw attention again later in the year by their coral-red berries. Where mass planting has been undertaken the effect is good.

Lime

Tilia cordata (Tiliaceae)   Perennial

The lime is a tree native to England and Wales, especially on limestones, and is planted in gardens and streets and in the great avenue at Hampton Court. Lime flowers have been used for generations to make a pleasant tisane and the tree has a place in European folklore medicine. At one time it seems to have been a cure-all administered for a wide range of complaints from feverish chills to chest congestion. But linden tea, as the tisane is known, is a certain remedy for headaches and for poor digestion. It carries the delicate scent of the lime flowers, a scent used in cosmetics such as soap to add a fresh sweetness.

Loosestrife

Lythrum salicaria (Lythraceae)   Perennial
Purple loosestrife

An invaluable perennial for planting in dampish places, purple loosestrife revels in the muddy banks of streams and ponds and loves moist soils. The type is not often seen: garden cultivars are usually grown and make a brilliant addition to the herb garden. They are richer and brighter in flower and the poker-like rose-purple flower spikes are a good contrast to many of the less robust herbs. 'Prichard Variety', 'Robert', 'Firecandle' and 'Brightness' are all reliable cultivars. 'Robert' is lower growing than the remainder and is ideal for the front of the border.

Loosestrife was used formerly in tanning leather, and in dilute quantities as an eye wash. It is said to be an excellent gargle and wound cleanser with an antibacterial action. Propagation is by division of the clumps in spring, and non-flowering shoots may be used as cuttings.

Lovage

Levisticum officinale (Umbelliferae)   Perennial
Indian dolphin

A hardy herbaceous perennial with lusciously healthy green leaves and yellowish green flowers in umbels in July and August, lovage offers a good substitute in cooking for celery, as a pot herb, adding a stronger flavour rather more nutty than that of celery. The young growth of both foliage and stems can be added to salads, with some discretion because of the potency of the flavour. Harvested in late summer, when ripe, the aromatic seed is useful to flavour bread and pastries or to sprinkle on boiled rice or boiled potato. The roots are edible but require to be stripped of their bitter skin to render them palatable.

Most soils are suitable, and lovage is shade-tolerant, provided it gets sunshine at some time of the day. Give it a moist spot if possible, with some humus-enriching material worked in well, and it will repay with good resilient stems. A handsome plant, frequently not recognised, it ought to be more widely cultivated in the herb garden for its lustrous foliage alone.

Propagation is by July sown seed, or the roots can be divided in late autumn after the top growth has died down. Attractive bronze shoots emerge in the spring.

Lovage at Michelham Priory in Sussex.

Lungwort

Pulmonaria officinalis (Boraginaceae)   Perennial

Jerusalem cowslip, soldiers and sailors, lung moss

Lungwort is cultivated in many gardens for its spotted foliage and its flowers, which come at the same time as primroses and change colour so that there are always pink and blue ones together. Lungwort has been grown for centuries for its foliage, which contains mucilage, effective in the treatment of coughs and colds. Spring leaves can be chopped and added to salads and resemble borage in that they are of a cucumber flavour.

Choose a shaded area with good moisture-retentive soil and lungwort will be a good ground-cover plant. It forms extensive patches in woodland conditions and when the more silver-leaved species (*Pulmonaria saacharata*), sometimes called Bethlehem sage, is grown it can light up the ground beneath shrubs in a darkish corner. While this species is not strictly a herb it begs a place in the decorative herb garden.

Propagation is by division of roots in late summer after flowering. Once the flowers are over the growth tends to die down and fresh basal rosettes of leaves are formed. These are the pieces to separate. Spring division is also reliable when the ground can be worked early in the season, but many springs are either too wet or too cold for this operation to be successful in all but the milder districts. But lungwort tends to seed itself quite freely. If seedlings are not required it is advisable to remove old flowerheads.

Mace, English

Achillea decolorans (Compositae)   Perennial

The mace of commerce is derived from the dried outer seedcase of the nutmeg (*Myristica fragrans*). English mace is totally inferior, but the vernacular name simply pays homage to the fact that the flavour is hot, spicy and pungent. The plant has come to be known in some localities as the nutmeg plant. Leaves of this mace can be added to soups and stews or goulash-type dishes just to lend a dash of flavour.

The cream daisy flowers in June and July are of no special interest and the foliage is dark green and deeply divided. Mace is not often seen in cultivation but worthy of a place in the culinary herb collection. Propagation is by division in spring or autumn, and the pieces should be planted into a moderately rich soil in an open but sheltered spot. Where the soil is not sufficiently rich the foliage tends to become rather rank. It dries well and retains its pungency. The crowns may need to be protected in cold seasons or harsh areas, but by taking cuttings in July plants can be easily maintained in a frame or with some other slight protection in unfavourable areas.

Mallow

Malva sylvestris (Malvaceae)   Biennial
Cheeses

   The common mallow is a wild plant in Britain and strictly a biennial although it often forms a woody base and behaves as a short-lived perennial. Mauve-pink flat-faced flowers, each petal sketched with fine lines, are tucked among the soft rounded lobed leaves. Formerly used as a mild laxative, the seed heads, known as 'cheeses' because of their shape, can be added fresh to salads.

   Propagation is from seed, sown in the early summer and the straggly little mallow plants that result look best tucked among the stonework of steps or a retaining wall.

   For medicinal purposes it has largely been replaced by the marsh mallow (*Althea officinalis*) with softer-textured foliage and rather pinker flowers in later summer. Tolerant of sun and wind, this mallow is a good maritime plant provided that it is growing in moisture-retentive material. Again, the flattened seed heads can be eaten fresh. The foliage is a good salad ingredient when young and fresh or

Mallow.

a useful addition to stews or vegetable broths when older. An infusion of dried leaves is refreshing as a tea or a soothing eye bath. There is a long tradition of using marsh mallow as a soothing treatment for coughs and chest complaints in the form of a syrup. It is the roots that are used to combat inflammation of the digestive tract.

It is good plant for the back of the border in the herb garden. The flowers retain a translucent quality on drying and are said to add their rose colouring to wine. Propagation is from seed sown in spring to produce stout rich spires of flower the following season.

Marigold

Calendula officinalis (Compositae)   Annual
Pot marigold, marygold

The golden marigold needs no introduction even to the town dweller, and it is the most reliable of summer flowering annuals. Seedsmen offer a range of forms, all of them double-flowered, in a variety of yellow and orange shades. But the true official plant is a small single-flowered daisy, with a single row of pale orange-yellow ray petals and sometimes with a slightly darker central zone.

The flowers and leaves of this plant, and indeed of all garden cultivars, add flavour to salads or soups. But unless

Marigold.

the leaves are very young they are acrid and unacceptable to some palates. Flower petals make a pretty garnish to meat platters, pâté and fruit salad and add colour to curd cheese or a piquancy to yoghurt.

Numerous recipes including marigold can be discovered in old household books, and it was even believed that only to look upon marigolds strengthened the eyesight and 'withdrew evil humours out of the head'. The mucilage extracted from the whole plant has a healing action; marigold ointment was an old household remedy. A lotion made from the extraction restored the complexion, or a mixture of the extraction and cold cream made a perfect cleansing cream.

Sow the seed in spring in a sunny spot preferably in a fine loam, but the marigold is tolerant of a wide range of soils provided there is no waterlogging. For window-boxes, tubs and other containers sow *in situ*. In the summer some plants will develop a fibrous base and overwinter, especially in sheltered places. Self-sown seedlings usually inhabit the garden too, once marigolds have been introduced. In dry areas autumn-sown seed provides good plants for effect as early as May the following year.

Marjoram

Origanum species (Labiatae)   Perennial

All marjorams have a strong warm flavour in their leaves, and to some extent in the flowers. Sweet or knotted marjoram (*Origanum majorana*) is a perennial plant from the warm countries around the Mediterranean, and so in cooler climates, such as Britain's, it is usually treated as an annual. Rather rougher in flavour and much hardier, pot marjoram (*Origanum onites*) is the plant more usually grown, simply because it will tolerate the dampness more easily.

Marjoram.

Golden marjoram.

Both plants produce small twiggy stems, brittle to the touch and bedecked with aromatic leaves. Pot marjoram has either white or pink flowers in midsummer; sweet marjoram always has pink flowers. Various leaf forms are to be found, some with a golden yellow splash across one corner of the leaf, others with golden leaves, and others, less aromatic, with pure gold leaves – very useful for the decorative herb garden, where they can be well used to form the edge of a bed or border.

Used as a flavouring since ancient times, the marjorams were also in demand for strewing in public places and dwellings. Flower tops can be used to decorate salads or garnish meat dishes, or they can be sprinkled into cooling drinks in summer. It is the leaves that are used mainly, in both French and English cookery, often in conjunction with thyme – which marjoram strongly resembles in flavour – as a constituent of *bouquet garni*.

Wild marjoram (*Origanum vulgare*) is known as oregano and grows wild all over Europe, including Britain. (In some countries, notably Mexico and the southern United States, oregano is a colloquial name for unrelated plants, which have a similar flavour.) It is wild marjoram, especially that of southern Europe, where the flavour is more biting than from the British plants, that gives the characteristic flavour to the Neapolitan pizza and is commonly used in the preparation of cold stuffed meats and sausages.

All the marjorams dry well for winter use, and all can be incorporated in pot-pourri – either flowers or leaves.

Propagation is from seed, sown in spring, or, for pot and wild marjoram, cuttings can be taken in early summer or the plants divided in the autumn. The wild marjoram is a more sprawling plant, which is best cut back in autumn to overwinter and form new shoots again the following spring. Marjorams all like to have plenty of sunshine and good soil; well grown plants are superior in flavour to those that are cultivated in shade or in dry soils.

Meadowsweet

Filipendula ulmaria (Rosaceae)   Perennial
Queen of the meadow, meadwort

Our ancestors knew this plant for its pain-dulling and cheering properties. The rich honey almond scent is easily communicated to liquids, so meadowsweet was a traditional flavouring for mead. It was scattered at

Meadowsweet.

weddings for its cheering, soporific action and it was the forerunner of aspirin. Formerly the plant was known as *Spiraea ulmaria* and aspirin means 'from spiraea'. It is interesting to note that for centuries meadowsweet was used to alleviate all the ailments for which today we seek aspirin: headaches, gout, menstrual discomfort and rheumatic joints.

Select a dampish soil for it in the garden and grow it at the water's edge where its upright stems are decorated with frothy clusters of cream flowers from midsummer onward. The dark green leaves with strongly toothed margins have quite a different scent from the flowers, which changes as they fade or dry.

Melilot

Melilotus officinalis (Papilionaceae)   Biennial
Common melilot, hart's clover

Spikes of bright yellow pea flowers in midsummer, held in an elegant fashion on long spikes all over the bushy plant, are the chief delight of melilot. A tea made from the fresh flowers relieves indigestion and flatulence and the fresh leaves make a good poultice for aching joints. The almond-like fragrance commends the plant in the scented garden, where the bees love it. The fragrance remains on drying and, indeed, increases in the same way as that of woodruff because they both contain coumarin. This is why it has been used for generations as a fodder plant. It is now naturalised on waste land in many localities in Britain.

Propagation is from seed, and if this is sown early in the spring the plant will behave as an annual, coming into flower the same year, but if the seed is sown in high summer, melilot will overwinter and flower the following May and June.

Mignonette

Reseda odorata (Resedaceae)   Perennial
Little darling, sweet mignonette

Strictly a perennial but usually grown as an annual, mignonette was grown much more a century ago than it is today. It atones for its somewhat insignificant flower colour with a strong musky perfume. Modern plants suffer from the loss of much of the scent through cultivation, resulting in a lack of popularity. But in Victorian times the mignonette was a pot plant *par excellence,* used for parlour, greenhouse, conservatory and window-box decoration. Beloved of bees and useful for drying to add to pot-pourri, it can be grown in any sunny corner where the soil is light and firm. Flowers are reddish green in June and July and seedsmen are now offering 'sweet' varieties claimed to be fragrant.

The upright mignonette (*Reseda alba*) is sweetly scented of almond, more strongly than any other species. The leaves are particularly deeply divided and the flower spikes of small white flowers come in June. Often the plant behaves as a biennial or, at best, a very short-lived perennial.

Mint

Mentha species (Labiatae)   Perennial

Most people can recognise a few of the numerous species and forms of mint, which are an interesting tribe of plants, ranging from *Mentha requienii*, the smallest known plant in Britain, to *Mentha* x *villosa* 'Alopecuroides' Bowles's mint, with large hairy leaves. For culinary use the true pea mint flavour is needed and this mint has it, as has the common green lamb mint, *Mentha spicata*, the commonest mint of all.

Mentha spicata is the commonest mint.

Less confusion than in the past surrounds the names of mints, although some of the English names allocated in wayside nurseries are suspect. The principal mints to cultivate are:

Mentha aquatica 'Citrata', known colloquially as lemon mint simply because it has a cleaner flavour than *aquatica* itself, which is rather acrid. The leaves are rounded and shining green and suffused or tinted with purple when well grown in dampish soil. It is a somewhat variable plant with lilac or red flowers in rounded terminal heads.

Mentha x *gentilis* (ginger mint or spicy mint) has smooth green leaves strongly splashed with yellow or coral red. The whole plant appears to be more branched than the bolder mints and when first rubbed it emits a clean minty smell which soon become pungent or gingery. It is a hybrid between the wild *M. arvensis* and *M. spicata*.

Ginger mint.

Mentha x *piperita*, the popularly cultivated peppermint, is the plant from which oil of peppermint is obtained for use in pharmaceutical and confectionery flavouring. Peppermint tea, made from either fresh or dried leaves of this mint, is ready to drink in three or four minutes after infusion and is a refreshing aid to digestion. Plants with dark purple, almost bronze stems, go by the name of black peppermint, or those with much less colouration as white peppermint. The flowers are mauve in a terminal spike and are usually clustered round the stem in separate whorls below. This plant is a hybrid between *M. aquatica* (the water mint) and *M. spicata* (spearmint) and its forms vary in their scent. Thus *M.* x *p.* 'Citrata' has come to be known as bergamot mint or eau de Cologne mint, in which the bronze colouring is rubbed round the edge of the leaves and is more suffused over the plant and accompanied by a sharp lemon scent. Another form is *M.* x *p.* 'Crispa', in which the bases of the green leaves clasp the purple stem and have a fringed edge.

Mentha pulegium (pennyroyal) is a creeping plant, the stems of which root where they contact the soil, and which goes under the name of pudding grass. It makes its flower stems stand up as they mature, bearing separate bobbles of purplish mauve flowers up the stem. A form marketed as *M. p.* 'Upright' has been developed in which the prostrate character of the plant is minimised; this is catalogued as upright pennyroyal. There is a strong peppermint scent, good late in the summer because the plant does not flower until the early autumn.

Mentha spicata (spearmint, garden mint or pea mint of the kitchen garden) is by far the most widely grown. It is sometimes offered as Moroccan mint and if we recall that its former name was *M. viridis*, meaning green, it is easily distinguished from all other mint forms. Then look at the spear-shaped pointed leaf – there can be no mistake. A plant marketed as red raripila mint (or spearmint), *M. raripilia rubra* is closely akin to *M. spicata* in scent but has reddish brown stems and somewhat thicker leaves, sometimes with a red main vein.

Mentha suaveolens appears in catalogues with an array of name tags and various decorative forms, which include apple mint, pineapple mint or Egyptian mint. All have a distinctly fruity overtone to the minty aroma. For identification the leaves are oval or nearly round and

Apple mint, or woolly mint.

softer than the foregoing forms, and with downy stems. In its variegated leaved form *M. s.* 'Variegata' it is usually known as apple mint, with creamy white markings on the leaves and many young shoots breaking completely white or cream. It is a pretty edging plant for the flower border and a 'must' for the decorative herb garden, where it tends to lighten the effect. When allowed to flower the heads usually come in threes and are terminal, purplish mauve spikes which often curve when young. One characteristic strongly in its favour is that as a garden plant it persists longer into the winter than the other mints.

Mentha x *villosa*, another hybrid mint (*M. suaveolens* x *M. spicata*), is best known in its form 'Alopecuroides' or Bowles' mint, with broad, pale, somewhat woolly leaves that are very soft to the touch. The grandest and tallest of all the tribe, it can grow up to a metre in height with long purple flower spikes. Its vigour also pervades the flavour, which is superb for mint sauce. The hairy leaves may discourage some cooks from trying them but, once chopped, the hairiness disappears.

Within the genus there is a slight range of aroma resulting from the chemical composition of the essential oils within the fabric of the plant. Some nuances have led to many common names being used to describe various mint aromas. All the mints hybridise easily and vary in scent according to the conditions under which they are grown, and therefore a complicated array of plants is available. Remember that the aroma, and therefore the flavour, of a plant is at its richest and best just before flowering, and try not to use or harvest mint after flowering, because some of them become quite rank and are certainly inferior in herbal quality.

The soft leaves of all the mints dry fairly well but need special care to maintain a good clean colour as it is so easy for them to turn black. Try not to gather too many shoots at one time so that they can be well spread out to dry and thus dry properly. All the mints can be included in pot-pourri – the fruity ones are best – or put into sachets for storing in drawers and cupboards. Then if they are crushed or rubbed occasionally the dried leaves will release their aroma afresh. All of them can be used as an infusion, sometimes sweetened with honey to taste, known as mint ale.

All mints are propagated by pulling away a rooted runner. This is a good example of what the gardener calls an Irishman's cutting. The little runners planted out soon form new roots and are off to hunt territory of their own, for the mints are all great travellers. To restrain them, it is often necessary to contain them in an old bucket or tub sunk into the ground. Alternatively, the mint bed needs to be replanted every three years or so and often mint fails to grow because no thought has been given to the location of the bed. The unitiated gardener often believes that because a plant is commonly grown it is accommodating, and this is not always so. Remaking the mint bed disposes of the old stringy runners and overcomes the weeding problem to a considerable extent because once mint runners are established weeding is virtually impossible.

Monarda
see Bergamot

Motherwort
Leonorus cardiaca (Labiatae)   Perennial
Once established in ordinary soil where there is good light, motherwort survives the hardest winters because of its creeping underground stems. Tall square reddish stems

carry pairs of long, pointed, deeply veined leaves with purplish white flowers nestling in the axils. Since the seventeenth century its power as a fertility drug has been known and it is used homeopathically to reduce anxiety.

Mugwort

Artemisia vulgaris (Compositae)   Perennial
Felonwort, St John's herb, mother of herbs

Mugwort is an ancient plant, coarse and not particularly attractive, but one that links Anglo-Saxon herb lore with the present. It was one of the nine herbs depended upon to ward off demons and venomous creatures who lived in the great unknown. In the Middle Ages it was used for clarifying beer, but it is now known best for its appetite stimulating properties and as a general pick-me-up. This is the plant that has been used for centuries by the Chinese in the therapeutic treatment of rheumatism in moxibustion and is being used today in Britain in the treatment of some pregnancy problems.

A northern European native plant, it infests waste land quickly and in cultivation needs to be restrained and cut back ruthlessly because it grows very quickly up to 2 metres. It should be kept at the back of the border in the herb garden. Divide the plants in autumn for replanting. A variegated leaf form is in commerce but does not add anything to the attraction of the plant.

Mullein

Verbascum thapsus (Scrophulariaceae)   Biennial
Blanket weed, Aaron's rod, hag's taper

Mullein is a denizen of waste places, roadsides or other grassy places in Britain but has long been cultivated in cottage gardens. The unique characteristic of mullein is the rosette of large thick felt-like silver-white leaves. They diminish in size and number up the height of the stem and the tall yellow flower spike blooms in July and August. The general hairiness of the plant renders it susceptible to winter dampness and in some situations, where the drainage is poor, the leaves may need picking over or constantly brushing free of debris. Mullein seeds itself easily, so once introduced into the garden there is little need to ensure its continuance. Propagation, however, is from seed sown in summer, and the rosette will be formed the first season, the flower spike produced the second.

The leaves, collected especially in the first year, are used to make an infusion for the relief of pulmonary congestion, but the liquor needs to be meticulously strained to eliminate the hairs, which otherwise act as an irritant. The dried leaves are used as a herb tobacco. The down from the stems and leaves used to be stripped off and used as tinder and lamp wicks. The erect tall hairy stem, after dipping in tallow or suet, was used to make a torch or rush light, hence the name hag's taper.

Myrtle

Myrtus communis (Myrtaceae)   Woody perennial

Beautifully and richly aromatic in both leaf and flower, myrtle is a shrubby plant of ancient fame, dedicated to the goddess Venus and therefore considered to be an aphrodisiac. It is an evergreen that requires a sheltered spot or sunny corner with wall protection. It has glossy pointed leaves and powder-puff-like creamy white flowers in high summer, followed by bluish berries, if they ripen. The berries are dried and crushed, and the flower buds, treated in the same way, can be used as a spice. Leaves to accompany roast pork are added during the last ten minutes of cooking time.

Myrtle is not used medicinally although there are records of a decoction of the leaves being used to treat bruises, applied externally for the antiseptic qualities. Flowers or sprays of leaves and flowers are used symbolically to denote fertility and are thus added to bridal bouquets or used to garnish wedding buffets.

Nasturtium

Tropaeolum majus (Tropaeolaceae)   Annual

'Nasturtium' is a misnomer: the garden nasturtium, so easily recognised with its orange long-spurred flowers, bears the true Latin name of the watercress (*Nasturtium officinale*). The confusion has most likely arisen because of the peppery taste of the round leaves. These round leaves, held at right angles to the stem, can best be used by rubbing a broken leaf round the salad bowl to flavour a green salad. The seeds are sometimes included in pickles and chutneys, but this practice seems to be falling into disfavour. They are peppery in flavour.

Nasturtium.

Raise a fresh supply of plants each year, for decoration in the herb garden, or for containers such as window-boxes. There are trailing kinds and dwarf forms also. The nasturtium is a useful plant giving quick results, always encouraging in children's gardens. Unfortunately it seems to attract blackfly.

Nettle

Urtica dioica (Urticaceae)   Perennial

The nettle needs no description. It is one of the first plants children learn to recognise. The young leaves can be used in the spring as a green-leaf vegetable, known as 'nettle tops' and served like spinach, with a knob of butter or a sprinkling of caraway seed. The stinging hairs are rendered innocuous by boiling. An infusion of nettle leaves, fresh or dried, and sweetened with honey, gives some relief from bronchial congestion.

The rich minerals and iron in nettle leaves make them a valuable vegetable at a time of year when green leaves are in short supply. Expressed juice of the nettle acts as rennet, with salt, in forming curd cheese and junkets.

Nettle beer is an old cottage recipe as a remedy for gout and rheumatic pains, apart from being a pleasant drink. Rheumatic sufferers sometimes chastise themselves by thrashing the affected joints with freshly gathered nettle shoots. The effect is similar to the treatment of rheumatism by bee stings.

The fibre is similar to that of hemp and has been used in the past to make a range of cloths from the finest cambrics to utilitarian cordage and in the manufacture of paper.

Opium poppy

Papaver somniferum (Papaveraceae)   Annual

The abuse of the product of this plant has led to much human misery, but it has provided one of the greatest painkillers of all time – morphine. Its specific name, *somniferum*, means 'sleep inducing'. Its floppy pink to red flowers are a fine additon to the herb garden, standing well above the glaucous indented leaves. After flowering they dry to produce the 'poppy heads' that are popular with flower arrangers. Propagate from seed sown afresh each spring, although once introduced the plants will seed themselves provided that the soil is not too sticky and cold. In some parts of Britain this poppy is a common wild plant, and seed is readily available. There are double and single flowered forms, in pink, mauve and dull red.

Add it to a representative medicinal collection of herbs. The seed heads were formerly sold powdered to be used as an infusion for the relief of strains and bruised joints.

Orris

Iris florentina (Liliaceae)   Perennial
White flower de luce, Florentine iris

The white purple-veined flowers of *Iris florentina* bloom early in the summer and after flowering the flower stems should be cut back to encourage complete ripening of the root or rhizome – the source of orris. Once the roots are mature in August and September they can be lifted, washed free of soil and dried, after which they adopt the fragrance reminiscent of violets. When they are first lifted they are inodorous, but the scent develops and increases by keeping. This is why the chopped or ground root is so valuable in the making of pot-pourri because it absorbs the homogeneous aroma of all the other ingredients and helps to stabilise the whole perfume.

The plants reach some 60 cm in height and prefer a light soil and sunshine, but with some shade in the course of the day. Propagation is by division of rhizomes in July to September, preferably the former, when the task is much easier. By September more roots have grown, making the tangle more difficult to sort out properly.

Parsley

Petroselinum crispum (Umbelliferae)   Biennial

Parsley takes pride of place in British kitchens as a garnishing plant, and often one finds the garnish discarded at the end of the meal. Most people do not realise that the crisply curled leaves can be eaten as a salad. Apart from being chopped in the making of parsley sauce to serve with fish and boiled bacon, parsley is an ingredient in *sauce*

Parsley.

tartare and in *sauce verte*, and *bouquet garni* requires parsley stalk. French housewives tend to add a pinch or two of parsley in much the same way that the British housewife adds salt. The best forms to grow are the richly curly-leaved ones: they are richer in vitamins and iron as well as looking better at the table. Parsley does not dry well but can be frozen after blanching, and although when defrosted it is not so attractive for its usual rôle of garnishing it can be used in all the other ways.

It is a true biennial plant, originating from the regions around the Black Sea. It is best sown in April or May, either in rows or as an edging to garden beds, or even in blocks. Germination can be intolerably slow, and there is a belief that parsley goes nine times to the devil and back before germinating. It can be encouraged a little by soaking the seed overnight before sowing and running along the drill with a kettle of boiling water, just trickling from the spout, immediately before sowing the seed. Where good foliage is needed, do not allow the plants to flower or bolt.

Periwinkle

Vinca major (Apocynaceae)   Perennial
Sorcerer's violet

This is a procumbent shrubby trailing plant, which symbolically binds. As a garden plant it helps to stabilise banks, forming a tough ground cover, and as a herb of Venus it is said to bind people together. Its use as an aphrodisiac has been recognised since the fourteenth century. In times past it was used to stem the flow of blood and 'bind' the flesh of wounds. Even the manner in which its petals appear to spin in wheel fashion around the centre of the flower suggests the binding action. Binding also suggests protection and the periwinkle's past reputation for warding off evil spirits accounts for its English name of sorcerer's violet.

The variegated leaf form *V. major* 'Variegata' is a popular garden and container plant readily available in commerce. However, one or two other forms are well worth seeking out for the herb border, such as the smaller, less robust *V. minor* and its various flower forms: 'Azura Flora Plena', for example, with bright violet-blue double flowers, 'Caerulea Plena' with clearer blue double flowers, or 'Burgundy' with wine-purple single flowers, not unlike the type *V. minor atropurpurea*.

Purslane

Portulaca oleracea (Portulacaceae)   Annual

Purslane is a sprawling half-hardy plant that revels in sunshine. The reddish stems and clear green fresh leaves can be used in salads or steamed as a vegetable. Older leaves make a useful addition to stews and soups, and the stems are pickled, in sections, and used as a relish. Both this and *Portulaca sativa*, the golden purslane, are half-hardy annuals and should be sown out of doors in early May once the soil is warming up a bit. Keep the young plants growing, once they are established, by watering judiciously to ensure good quick growth and a better leaf texture. By pinching out the flower buds and preventing the plants from flowering, better leaf growth is maintained and the leaves are discouraged from becoming coarse. The golden purslane seems to need more encouragement, especially in poor summers, but is the more decorative plant to use for the table.

Rampion

Campanula rapunculus (Campanulaceae)   Biennial

Several plants seems to be tagged rampion, but the true one has hairbell-like deep blue flowers and is sometimes grown as an ornamental border plant. Previously rampion was cultivated regularly in the kitchen garden as a root vegetable, the root being lifted at the end of the second year. It was eaten cooked and served with a white sauce or sliced thinly and dressed with a vinaigrette as a salad accompaniment.

The rosette of leaves is formed the first summer, and if the plants are needed for use flower spikes must be prevented from forming in the second summer. By earthing up in the second spring the young leaves are rendered more tender, and it is reported that this also makes the roots a better flavour, preventing any light from coarsening the crown.

Rose

Rosa gallica officinalis (Rosaceae)   Shrub
Apothecary's rose

The long history of the rose centres around this lovely deep pink-red rose, and it is grown as popularly today as ever before. For pot-pourri these are the fragrant petals *par excellence* to gather, and for inclusion in some of the old recipes that are creeping back into use: rose petal jam, rose sorbet, rose vinegar etc.

Known as the Provins rose, it was in a town of that name to the south of Paris that it enjoyed the apogee of its fame, being cultivated there by the hectare for the production of rose perfumery items, conserves and sweetmeats, waters, vinegars, gateau, and in sachets, powders and papers and as crystallised petals that were exported widely.

For the herb garden there is no better hedge, as the shrubs planted about 70 cm apart will quickly form an impenetrable boundary or good breeze-sifting barrier. In its striped flowered form, *R. g.* 'Versicolor', it is known as Rosa Mundi. If ever Nature enjoyed a whimsical sense of fun it was surely in painting the peppermint rock pink stripes upon these blush pink flowers. Both plants give their perfume on to the air, to be carried across the garden on the breeze, so it is a first-rate plant for value in the herb garden.

Rosemary

Rosmarinus officinalis (Labiatae)   Perennial

Rosemary is said to have been a 'comforter of the brains and a strengthener of the memory'. The delicate blue flowers cover the plumes of dark green growth in early summer, and in early seasons or early districts can begin to flower in March. The plants are evergreen and decorative, reaching about 2 metres in height, and are useful as a hedge plant, although uneven in growth. They tolerate clipping. A sunny site with good drainage is ideal, but the plant is fairly accommodating and can be grown in containers, making it useful for porch plant arrangements in the colder areas. The foliage is richly resinous but has to be brushed with the hand to release the volatile oils.

Propagation is from cuttings of non-flowering shoots taken in early autumn and put under a cloche or in a sheltered frame to overwinter. Cuttings taken in spring are very successful and can often be encouraged to root in water.

When rosemary is used as a culinary herb, there will inevitably be some dissension. The flavour is too fierce for many palates, and for this reason it is best to use rosemary leaves after drying, when some of the pungency has been lost. A sprig or two are often pushed into lamb before

Rosemary at the Geffrye Museum in London.

roasting, to flavour it, but if a few sprigs are placed beneath the joint while cooking the flavour seems to pervade the whole joint, less strongly and perhaps more evenly. Rosemary leaves are always removed after cooking, and before serving the food, because they are tough and spiky.

Oil of rosemary used to be used as an embrocation for sprained or gouty joints and as an insect repellent. Its long association with hair cosmetics dates back many years to when it was considered effective as a hair restorer. For a refreshing bath, fasten a few sprigs of fresh rosemary into an old nylon stocking and hang it below the taps so that as the water runs into the bath it becomes scented with rosemary.

Always add a dried sprig to pot-pourri; it is one of the main ingredients, but never too much as its camphorous aroma can overpower any sweet-scented mixture.

Rue

Ruta graveolens (Rutaceae)   Perennial
Herb of grace
    The herb of repentance, rue is an evergreen sub-shrub

94

that forms a rounded bush, the foliage of which is very pungently bitter in aroma when crushed. Its only possible use as a healing herb nowadays is in the treatment of poultry. There is some association with witches and black magic as it was used in the treatment of epilepsy and considered to be a cure for insanity. But rue is an example of a herb being used on conditions that were not understood in the past, and because of its drastic effects in unpractised hands it was thought to possess supernatural powers.

In Tudor times it was commonly strewn in dwellings and public buildings, such as courtrooms, as a protection against evil. In the Middle Ages its powerful bitterness of flavour was used to mask putrefaction. A leaf or two only, finely chopped, can be added to cream cheese, but beware – a heavy hand with the rue is disastrous.

There are three forms to grow in the decorative herb garden: green, green-blue and variegated-leaved plants. The last form often proves difficult to keep as it reverts to its plain green form. The foliage is prettily cut and the four-petalled yellow flowers bloom in summer. Give it a sunny spot with good drainage, for, as with many other herbs from

Rue.

sunnier climes than Britain's, moisture encourages lush growth that is less hardy and inferior in aroma.

Saffron

Crocus sativus (Iridaceae)   Bulb

The saffron crocus is nowhere known in the wild although it is to be found as a relic of cultivation in some areas bordering the Mediterranean. Grown for centuries to provide a dye and colouring agent for food, and as a medicine and condiment, its cultivation is commemorated in such place names as Saffron Walden in Essex, where it was grown from the reign of Edward III.

It can only be increased by breaking off the daughter plants from the mother corm, then being grown in the herb garden as a plant representative of ancient cultivation. The brilliant yellow dye is obtained from the stigmas, thousands of which are needed to produce a small amount of true saffron yellow. Charlatans thrived on merchandising substitutes! It served also as a substitute for gold in illuminating manuscripts, when burnished upon tinfoil.

The plant is a true crocus, large with lilac-purple flowers shading to white and strongly veined, and the distinguishing feature is that the yellow stigmas flop sideways out of the flower almost as if they were bent or too heavy to support themselves. In general, herbs have a short period of interest as cultivated plants, starting late and finishing early in the season, so the saffron crocus, flowering in the autumn, is of little impact in the desolate garden.

Sage

Salvia officinalis (Labiatae)   Perennial

The culinary sage which is most commonly grown forms a somewhat floppy bush. The leaves are dusty grey in colour, wrinkled and pitted rather like orange peel in appearance, and rough in texture. The whole plant seems rather dry. The leaves are used in making stuffing for poultry and rich meats such as pork and should be gathered before the plant comes into flower. Sage is one of the few herbs that is not usually used fresh but is better dried, because the flavour is then less fierce. Sprigs of leaves can be cut and hung up in loose bunches to dry, in a warm dry atmosphere. Cover them with a piece of cloth or newspaper

Sage.

to keep the sun away if a shaded place cannot be found. Miraculously, sage leaves do not reabsorb moisture even if they are not dried completely.

Sage ale or beer, drunk cold, is said to dispel many varied ailments and to 'increase cheerfulness'. Sage tea was preferred by the Chinese to their own tea, of which they even bartered three times as much by weight for sage from Dutch merchants. It is made by pouring a litre of boiling water over 50 grams of dried sage leaves and flavouring with either lemon juice or lemon rind to taste, with a spoonful of honey stirred into it. John Evelyn wrote of it as possessing so many properties 'as that the assiduous use of it is said to render men immortal'. Another use of sage is in the flavouring of Derby sage cheese, when the whole cheese takes on a marbled appearance and a strong rough sage-like flavour. Burned in a chestnut roaster, sage smoke will deodorise animal and cooking smells. Crushed, it can be used as a tooth powder, for those who do not find the dryness of the flavour too strong, and used to remove tobacco and red wine stains from the teeth.

The primary requirement when selecting a sage bush for the garden, if the leaves are destined for culinary use, is to find a plant whose idiosyncrasies match the soil conditions. When sage is well suited to the spot in which it is required to grow, it will produce foliage completely devoid of any bitterness of flavour or 'flatness'. A little patience and trial and error are necessary in establishing the right sage bush in the kitchen garden.

Propagation is from summer cuttings taken with a heel, or by layers pegged down in summer and severed and planted out the following spring.

The coloured leaved forms are not the ones to grow for culinary use but they do add considerable interest to the decorative herb garden. Be prepared to replace them fairly frequently by keeping a stock of rooted cuttings or layers as they seem to be of weaker constitution than *S. officinalis*. They are invaluable for providing colour contrast, especially for troughs and other containers.

S. icterina is of much sweeter flavour than *officinalis*, forming a low growing gentler shrub with narrow golden leaves. Give it a sunny corner in the border and it will respond and live up to its name of golden sage. Try it in turkey stuffing.

S. officinalis 'Purpurascens' provides a good planting contrast with its deep plum-purple foliage – which incidentally makes a pretty garnish for cold meats and vegetable dishes.

S. o. 'Tricolor' has, as its name suggests, leaves that are splashed and daubed in various combinations of purple, pink, green and cream. No wonder it is called painted sage. When a pleasing clone is found, it is to be treasured and propagated because it adds a festive air to the garden. The whole plant seems softer than the form *S. officinalis*.

Purple sage.

Decorative sage 'Tricolor'.

S. rutilans, the pineapple sage, is a different plant altogether, and is tender. It is only successful in sheltered gardens and away from cold winds and winter dampness, although it can be maintained from a regular supply of

Broad-leaved sage 'Berggarten'.

cuttings. The leaves are highly aromatic of pineapple when crushed or rubbed, and deep red flowers are produced in the late summer or even early autumn. It makes a good conservatory or porch plant, where the aromatic leaves can be enjoyed in passing.

Salad burnet

Poterium sanguisorba, Syn *Sanguisorba minor* (Rosaceae)

Perennial

Salad burnet is a pretty and hardy plant, sometimes found wild in Britain, whose leaves remain green in winter. In the garden it makes an attractive edging to beds and its small rounded heads of reddish green flowers at midsummer earn it the local name of blood ball. Remove the flowers to encourage leaf production and maintain a continuous supply of dainty cucumber-flavoured leaves to add to salads. There is no aroma to the leaves.

It was used as a herb in medieval times. The leaves may be chopped and added to cream cheese or summer drinks to impart the somewhat crisp flavour likened to that of cucumber skin. The individual leaves need to be removed from the pink stems, but when used for garnishing the colour contrast is an added attraction.

Santolina

see Lavender cotton

Savory

Satureia species, sometimes *Satureja* (Labiatae)

Annual and perennial

There are two distinct forms of savory: the winter savory, which is a perennial, *Satureia montana*; and an annual plant, *Satureia hortensis*. Neither seems to be widely grown or much used. The flavour is similar to that of an old thyme, rough, peppery and sharp, especially in winter savory. Propagate winter savory by cuttings or by division of roots in autumn or spring, and a plant can be left for five years before it will require to be replaced. The annual savory can be raised from seed sown in April. Two or three crops can be taken from it and it stands up to clipping fairly well. It is widely used as a seasoning in European cookery to flavour gravies and sauces to accompany meat and is said to aid digestion and reduce flatulence. It used

Winter savory.

to be the substitute for pepper in past centuries, when pepper was prohibitive in price. It is often said to be served in a sauce with beans, but there seems little evidence of such use.

Sea holly

Eryngium maritimum (Umbelliferae) Perennial
Eryngo

The sea holly is a thistle-like plant, with jagged blue-grey leaves, spiked with sharp thorny edges, and protective little prickly leaves surrounding the metallic blue flowerheads. The plants are grown for their roots, which are long and rich in minerals. They used to be a popular sweetmeat and can be candied in the autumn to add to desserts as a sweetening agent or as a flavouring for jams and jellies. Young flowering shoots are said to be eaten in the same way as asparagus, the prickles being rendered innocuous by boiling.

Sea holly is a lovely plant to grow where there is plenty of sunshine and a light soil, where it has space to spread out unhampered by leafy neighbours.

Propagation is by root division in the autumn or from autumn-sown seed.

Selfheal

Prunella vulgaris (Labiatae)   Perennial
Sicklewort, hook heal, proud carpenter

Known as a common weed of cultivated and meadow land throughout the western world, its ubiquitous presence led in the past to its ready availability as a handy remedy for wounds. Some common names testify the faith that was vested in its healing powers – touch and heal for example sounds like magic.

The creeping rhizomes cover the ground, producing from midsummer well into autumn upright flower spikes of violet purple or sometimes pink flowers with pronounced purple calyces. They are held in distinctive squarish heads. It will appear unheralded in some gardens – herbalists grow many weeds! But if a pleasing form is found it ought to be included in a representative collection. It needs to be set at the front of the border where its spread can be monitored.

Soapwort

Saponaria officinalis (Caryophyllaceae)   Perennial
Bouncing Bet, fuller's herb, latherwort, crowsoap

It was William Turner in the sixteenth century who gave vernacular names to several wild plants where none was

Soapwort.

known previously, naming this plant soapwort. Evidence suggests that from ancient times its detergent property has been employed to clean fabrics. Fresh leaves and stems agitated in water provide the perfect medium for cleansing antique or delicate fabrics.

Tolerant of poor soil, the soapwort provides a pretty pink-flowered patch in the herb border from midsummer onwards. Propagation is by division of rootstock. The flowers are borne in clustered heads and are prettiest in the double-flowered form. It is recorded as having been used in the treatment of skin and some respiratory complaints.

Solomon's seal

Polygonatum multiflorum (Liliaceae) Perennial

The hybrid *P. multiflorum* x *odoratum* is probably the most common representative of the genus in gardens today, sold as *P. multiflorum*. Traditionally Solomon's seal was cultivated for its creeping rootstock which provides an astringent tonic useful for bathing black eyes. Gerard proclaimed its healing powers for bumps and bruises: 'the roots of Solomon's Seal stamped while fresh and green and applied taketh away in one night or two at the most, any bruise black of blew spots gotten by fals or womens wilfulness in stumbling upon their hastie husband's fists, or such like.' He recommended it highly for knitting bones as 'there is not another herb to be found comparable to it'.

For centuries the plant has been reputed to clear freckles and maintain a beauty to the skin. It holds a fabulous aura, unlike any other plant, with its graceful arching

Solomon's seal.

pale green stems stretching to 60 cm and bearing oval
leaves along the top half like wings above dangling waxy
bell flowers. Select dappled shade for it in the garden with
a moisture-retentive soil, for it is a plant of the woods and
needs some leaf mould from time to time. Propagation is
from division just after the stems die down in the autumn.

Sorrel

Rumex acetosa (Polygonaceae)

Perennial treated as annual

The sorrel grown in our gardens is a good and cultivated
form of the wild sorrel, *Rumex acetosa*. It is known also as
garden or common sorrel and occasionally even called
broad-leaved sorrel. Inevitably there is some confusion
because both wild and garden plants are called French
sorrel by various authorities.

It is a perennial plant with broad arrow-shaped leaves
and spikes of clustered tiny red-brown flowers in summer.
The tangy flavour of the leaves is its main culinary attribute
but it is only at its best before the plant flowers. So where

Sorrel.

the leaves are habitually used as salading, it is advisable to nip out the flower buds as soon as they begin to form. The flavour of the leaves is appreciated more by the French than anyone else, and recipes using sorrel can be found in books on French cookery. Sorrel soup is good, or the leaves can be wrapped around meat to tenderise it or around minced and risotto mixtures in the way that vine leaves are used. As an addition to salad, the leaves ought to be chopped and are especially well matched to tomato. Try a sorrel leaf in sandwiches with cold meat, for a refreshing flavour.

Propagation is by seed sown in drills, as for most salad crops, the seedlings being thinned subsequently. At all costs, the plants must be prevented from bolting, and by growing a few in a shaded situation a supply of less coarse leaves will always be available.

Rumex scutatus is a smaller plant altogether, sometimes called the buckler-leaved sorrel, and is lax of habit or even with trailing stems. The leaves are small and a paler green, and their flavour is not so good.

Note: large doses are poisonous, and sorrel should not be used by anyone predisposed to kidney stones, arthritis, rheumatism, gout or gastric acidity.

Southernwood

Artemisia abrotanum (Compositae)   Perennial
Old man, lad's love

The rather gnarled and dead appearance of this little bush in winter has gained it the name of the old man, but it is the most delightful addition to any herb or fragrant garden. Its soft green feathery foliage is silky to the touch and almost invites one to play with it to release the sweet camphor aroma. The foliage can be dried and added to mixed herbs for scenting cupboards and drawers, or a sprig can be put into a pot-pourri mixture. Plant it where it will be away from the summer winds and where it has some moisture-retentive material around its base. Cut it back early in the spring to encourage fresh growth in summer. It is a non-flowering plant.

Sunflower

Helianthus annuus (Compositae)   Annual

Apart from assuming dramatic proportions, and

Sunflower.

therefore to be out of scale in some gardens, the sunflower has a charismatic quality and a happy face that seems almost to watch what is taking place. Well named for the shape and colour of its flowers that mimic the sun, it also turns its face to the sun all day long. All parts of the plant are useful: the pith is one of the lightest substances known and is used in scientific work; the seed is a commercial commodity for oil extraction and for foodstuffs and pharmaceutical products. The plant has a remarkable ability to absorb water from the soil in huge quantities and has been utilised in the reclamation and improvement of marshy land.

The seed itself is a nutritive, being sprinkled on salads and soups, and can be nibbled with drinks, or it may be roasted and ground for use as a coffee substitute. The unopened flower buds make an interesting spring vegetable, if one can resist the temptation to allow the plants to flower and dominate the garden. The rough stems stripped of the outer strings will burn as candles –

especially safe out of doors for barbecue parties. The stalks have been used in paper making. Sunflower leaves make good fodder, or when dried serve as an ingredient of tobacco, giving a cigar-like flavour.

Select a sunny spot in the garden, sheltered from the prevailing winds for best effect, and grow plants *in situ* from seed sown in late spring or early summer when the frosts have passed. Do not transplant, then watch these splendid plants attain a height of anything up to 3.5 metres.

Sweet Cicely

Myrrhis odorata (Umbelliferae)   Perennial

The leaves of sweet Cicely are soft and lacy in texture, the growth appearing early in the spring. Tiny white flowers in May are carried in umbels like those of its numerous relatives and are followed by large black seeds, which have a flavour slightly like that of licorice. Try them scattered on creams and ice cream or, when unripe, added to salads. The foliage is sweet in flavour and makes a good addition to diabetic diets. It can be stewed with gooseberries or rhubarb or, for its lightness of flavour, chopped into a green salad, with restraint. The leaves do not dry.

Sweet Cicely.

Tansy

Tanacetum vulgare (Compositae)   Perennial

Tansy was used as one of the stewing herbs, because of its insecticide and deodorant qualities, and the dried leaves used to be kept among clothes and in bedding to repel fleas and lice. A loose bunch of tansy leaves hung up in a larder will discourage flies, or tansy leaves rubbed over meat covers will avert the attentions of blowflies.

Formerly it was a popular cleansing spring tonic, and tansy tea or tansy wine was always taken to tone up the system after the stodgy food of the winter. Habitually it was eaten at Easter, mainly in tansy cake or tansy pudding, known as 'tansies', commemorating the bitter herbs of the Passover. It is too strong for most palates and is now not generally recommended for use internally.

As an infusion, the leaves make a good soothing lotion for bathing aching or bruised joints and sprains, or as a treatment for varicose veins.

Cultivation is so easy that a gardener might better be advised to keep tansy at bay and constantly pull away the wandering roots. It will march across the garden: whichever spot is chosen for it, it will prefer to be elsewhere. It is a tough-growing perennial plant; the stems are so tough that they cannot be picked easily by hand, but require to be cut with secateurs.

Tansy.

Tarragon.

Tarragon

Artemisia dracunculus (Compositae)   Perennial
Estragon

The true French tarragon is a superior culinary herb, very useful in giving a blunt bite and heightening the flavour of other herbs. At its best it is used in the more sophisticated cookery, being added to egg dishes, fish, tomatoes, herb butters and cream soups. It is perhaps most familiar in tarragon vinegar, where fresh sprigs are put into a bottle filled with white wine vinegar. Allow it to remain for a couple of months, shaking occasionally. Stems to be used in this way are best gathered in the early part of the summer, when the essential oils in the plant are at their best and richest in flavour. Tarragon does not dry well, so it will need to be quick-frozen if it is needed for winter use. Whenever it is not fresh, there is a tendency for the flavour to become somewhat stale.

It is a southern European plant and therefore loves warmth, so grow it in a sunny spot where the drainage is good, to prevent lush growth forming. Otherwise it will succumb to the damp British winter.

Russian tarragon, *Artemisia dracunculoides*, has an inferior flavour and is not recommended for culinary use, although it ought to be included in the collection of culinary herbs for completeness.

Thyme

Thymus species (Labiatae)   Perennial

Thyme is one of the primary culinary herbs and provides a powerful aroma which is retained after the sprigs are either dried or frozen. One of the ingredients of *bouquet garni*, it can survive long slow cooking and because of its persistent fierceness is usually used in cooking as a dried sprig, then removed before serving the dish. The true culinary thyme is *T. vulgaris*, although for the herb garden there is a wide choice of other forms.

All thymes need a non-acid soil and sharp drainage and as much light as possible. Where they thrive they are invaluable as edging plants, and they may even be allowed to flow over the edge on to the path. Propagation is from spring or early summer sown seed or tip cuttings taken from established plants before they flower in summer. All the thymes are attractive to bees.

Universally thymes are marketed by their cultivar name

Thyme.

Thyme in flower.

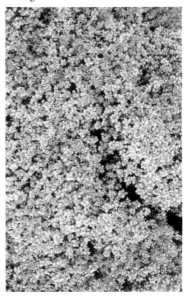

and catalogues from reputable nurseries should be consulted. Popularly grown ones are: 'Doone Valley', golden splashed foliage and a lemon scent; 'E. B. Anderson', golden foliage; 'Goldstream', lemon-scented with variegated leaves; and 'Lemon Curd', grey-green leaves with the lemon scent. All these have tiny lilac flowers while 'Snowdrift' has white flowers and pale green foliage. 'Porlock' and 'Silver Posie' are taller, both with pink flowers, and the latter has prettily variegated leaves that give a frosty look to the whole plant.

A serious collector of thymes would do well to visit one of the NCCPG National Plant Collections (see page 133) because many are catalogued under 'garden' names that have slipped into common use and have no botanical validity. The best species for the collector are:

T. caespititius (*azoricus*): a hummock-forming plant with pine-scented foliage and tiny purplish pink flowers. The whole plant is minute.

T. x *citriodorus* (*T. pulegioides* x *T. vulgaris*): a lemon-scented spreading little bush with smooth green leaves; in its 'Variegatus' form the leaves are edged with silver.

T. herba barona: the caraway-scented thyme; it is mat forming, straggles over the ground and has purple flowers.

T. polytrichus: the flowers are borne in great profusion in various shades of purple, differing with the clone.

T. pulegioides: the broad-leaved thyme, this has a strong flavour and a leaf larger than the common thyme.

T. serpyllum: known as the mother of thyme, this is the English wild thyme and is commonly encountered in various cultivars for gardens such as 'Annie Hall', with flesh-pink flowers. 'Coccineus', with particularly dark foliage, and 'Snowdrift', already listed as one of the best to grow, are *T. s.* ssp. *lanuginosus*.

T. vulgaris (common thyme or garden thyme) forms a cushion-like mound of growth; all other thymes form a carpet-like matted growth over the ground. A little hummock will reach about 30 cm in height and the cultivars are nearly the same: 'Aureus' with yellowish green leaves and 'Variegata' having a grey green appearance. All of them have tiny pale lilac flower heads in summer. Common thyme has the most pronounced medicinal qualities for its thymol content providing a strong antiseptic and it is widely used in pharmaceutical and cosmetic preparations. An infusion of fresh or dried sprigs is reputed to be a digestive tonic useful for hangovers.

Valerian

Valeriana officinalis (Valerianaceae)   Perennial
Phew, phu plant

A herb of ancient cultivation known to Arab physicians, valerian was grown for its useful rootstock, still listed in some pharmacopoeias. The root is roughly conical, with fibrous creeping offshoots when matured at the end of the summer. It is not lifted until about November when all the top growth has died down, for as long as this is green it is helping to enrich and mature the root. Once lifted, the roots need to be washed free of soil, and if they are bruised they develop an offensive smell, which has earned the plant its vernacular name of 'phew'. The smell is likened to that of old leather and is said to attract vermin and cats.

Grown in the herb garden, for its pretty, tall flowering stems with trimly cut leaflets, it is a good plant for the back of the border. Put it where it will get some shade during

Valerian.

the day, or in the dappled light beneath overhanging trees.

The flowers are very pale pink, in tight clustered heads in midsummer. The whole plant has a slightly foetid smell, but if it is at the back of the border there will be no temptation to touch it in passing, and its upstanding decorative quality certainly earns it a place in the herb garden. Propagate it by dividing the rootstock – and tolerating the smell for a few minutes.

This is not the plant so commonly grown as valerian, *Centranthus rubra*, of coastal regions.

Veratrum

Veratrum album (Liliaceae)   Perennial
White hellebore

At first glance this plant is sometimes confused with the yellow gentian, but a distinguishing feature is that the ribbed pleated leaves of the veratrum are alternate up the stem, whereas the gentian has opposite leaves. It is a statuesque plant, upstanding and quite imposing with its broad leaves and greenish white flowers in summer. This and the other hellebores (green and black) are strong poisons, formerly thought to have magical powers and surrounded by fear and superstitions. They have all been used as a dip for poison arrows. All of them irritate the skin and can cause blistering, but *album* especially is a dramatic plant to include in a herb garden. It needs a fairly well worked deep soil with some moisture-retentive material down at the roots and, once established, will look after itself.

Verbena
see Lemon verbena

Vervain
Verbena officinalis (Verbenaceae)   Perennial

Vervain has long been associated with magic and sorcery and came to be one of the most important sacred herbs, used in the making of holy salves. Its somewhat washed-out lilac flowers, appearing intermittently from about June to September in spikes, have little decorative quality, but vervain has a place in collections because of the medical folklore associated with it.

As a soothing wash for bruising or to cool the forehead in times of sickness, it is still used. An infusion is sometimes recommended for washing wounds.

The Victorians seem to have used it widely for a variety of home remedies, not least as a hair tonic. One of the first proprietary hair tonics to be marketed was made from vervain. Herbalists used to sell it as a soothing eye wash, especially for scrofulous eye conditions.

Violet
Viola odorata (Violaceae)   Perennial
Sweet violet

The violet has been a symbol of constancy since ancient times, when it was used as an officinal plant and as a cosmetic – the dye was used to paint the eyelids. In the nineteenth century it was one of the most popular of flowers used in love tokens, and Napoleon is said to have bestowed a nosegay of violets upon Josephine for each wedding anniversary.

Over the centuries, the leaves have formed poultices and dressings for ulcers and wounds of different kinds and have been used as a cure for insomnia, gout, cardiac complaints, a soothing remedy for headaches, a laxative, a treatment for catarrh and bronchitis, a gargle for sore throats, and in the relief of rheumatic pains – in fact it seems to have been a general cure-all.

Flowers can be candied and used in confectionery, and the favourite French *vyolette* became a recipe used in England at the time of the Restoration; macerated boiled violet flowers were used to impart colour to rice flour, which was then boiled with milk and sugar. Sometimes this is known as 'violet paste' and was supposed to be endowed with remarkable health-giving properties.

Before synthetic perfumes were manufactured following the First World War, violet water and sweet violet perfume were among the most popular scents, although often adulterated by the rhizome of the Florentine iris, *Iris florentina*. It is remarkable that at first the flowers smell sweet, and then the fragrance fades immediately. This is because it virtually anaesthetises the nasal nerves.

In the garden, sweet violets like best to be left to themselves in a shady bank, just as in their wild state. They are stoloniferous and mat-forming where they are happy.

Welsh onion

Allium fistulosum (Liliaceae)   Perennial
Ciboule

Where winters are severe Welsh onions need to be treated as an annual raised from spring sown seed or even as biennials from summer sown seed. Otherwise clumps should be divided and replanted elsewhere in a sunny spot, or the strain deteriorates.

A striking, upstanding form of onion, it has strongly flavoured 'evergreen' leaves up to 60 cm long which are hollow and usually swell towards the base into a flattened bulb. 'Welsh' means foreign, as the plant is not indigenous to Wales, but to China and Japan, although it is now not known anywhere in the wild. It provides good

Welsh onion.

115

flavour for salads and dips when the leaves are chopped, or they may be added to stews and broths.

Wintergreen

Gaultheria procumbens (Ericaceae)   Perennial
Checkerberry, mountain tea

While the name wintergreen conjures up pharmaceutical associations, wintergreen oil is now a synthetically produced commodity, and there is scant evidence that it was ever much used from this plant, the main source being *Betula lenta*.

As a small creeping evergreen shrub *Gaultheria* can justifiably be included in the representative herb collection, but more especially for its value as a plant for poor and acid soils. An infusion of the leaves, fresh or dried, may be used as a gargle, or to bathe swollen joints because the clean smelling oil is readily absorbed by the skin. (Pure oil may irritate some skins.)

Stiff erect branches about 15 cm long stand up from the creeping stems, with shining green leaves, pale beneath, and small white flowers like tiny lily-of-the-valley flowers dangle beneath in late summer, followed by freely produced red berries.

Woad

Isatis tinctoria (Cruciferae)   Biennial
Dyer's woad

The blue dye obtained from the woad plant seems surprisingly inappropriate, for the plant has profuse bright yellow flowers. The dye known from ancient times is obtained by fermenting the bruised leaves, but nowadays its use as a wool dye has been superseded. However, leaves picked the first year of growth can be put to use.

Grow woad from seed sown in autumn as soon as it is ripe. In good summers, the rich black seeds ripen beautifully in southern British gardens, decking the plant with shining black beads. It germinates easily, develops into a good rosette the first year and flowers the second.

Woodruff

Galium odorata (Rubiaceae)   Perennial
A plant of the woods and other shaded localities, woodruff has white star-like flowers and a straggling habit.

Woodruff.

Once dried, it takes on the scent of new-mown hay, which strengthens with time. For this reason alone it is invaluable as an ingredient of pot-pourri, scented sachets and herb pillows. It is also useful to spread about in closed bookcases to remove and avoid mustiness. The persistent scent means that woodruff can be used as a perfume fixative.

Propagation is by division of the running roots, in autumn. It can look rather weedy when not in flower but is such a simple plant that no garden should be without a patch.

Wormwood

Artemisia absinthium (Compositae)   Perennial
Absinth, green ginger

One of the loveliest plants in the herb garden, wormwood is so named for its internal worm-expelling properties. The pale silver-green, deeply cut foliage is soft and at its very best after rain, when it is decorated by jewelled raindrops, or in moonlight, when it seems to reveal some of the secrets of its magical past.

It forms a rounded small bushy plant with a woody base and should be cut right back in autumn to provide luscious attractive foliage the following spring.

It is very bitter in flavour, having the reputation of being the most bitter herb, exceeding even rue. However, it compensates in fragrance with a sweet camphor-like scent and it dries well, retaining a considerable scent. Scatter it among linen or add a sprig to pot-pourri or to a tussie-mussie.

Yarrow

Achillea millefolium (Compositae)   Perennial

Milfoil, carpenter's grass, old man's pepper, sneezewort

The feathery, somewhat dusty foliage of yarrow constitutes one of the commonest of wayside weeds of northern Europe, and of the temperate regions of the entire world. The flat clustered daisy-like flowers held in little heads are chalk-white or pinkish, and often the entire plant enshrouds itself in a veil of dustiness. The stems are so tough that they cannot be plucked by hand without difficulty; in fact they will cut the skin but also stem the flow of blood. Here is the clue to the vernacular names, for it will stop bleeding from a wound, or nosebleeding or fluxes. Conversely it has been used to cause excessive sneezing to induce nosebleeds to relieve headaches.

The aromatic oils give it a slightly nutty fragrance that pervades an infusion, making a herb tea of pleasing flavour, and used for fatigue, cystitis, incontinence and dysentery or combined with elderflower and peppermint for colds and influenza… a very comprehensive herb! An ointment made from it is used in the treatment of suppurating ulcers and varicose veins.

When dried the leaves retain their aroma and thus are an ingredient of herbal tobaccos. Try a sprinkling of fresh chopped leaves in salads and dips to add a peppery flavour: use with restraint.

Spring sown seed will soon produce flowering plants which later need to be divided and controlled. It is a good ground cover plant.

Its powers seem legion. It is reputedly a compost activator in the garden, so that one leaf per wheelbarrow load of garden rubbish to be composted will speed decomposition. That is real magic!

Cooking with herbs

Herbs in various proportions, alone or in a mixture, are used in culinary practice to enhance flavour, to garnish, or to aid the digestion of rich dishes. It is essential to use some herbs fresh – or, if not, at least to accept that when they are frozen or dried their effect will be inferior to that of the fresh form. Such culinary herbs are fennel, chervil, parsley and basil. When mint is to be used to make mint sauce there is no possibility of using dried leaves but, on the other hand, when dried it is used in stuffings, pilaffs or soups to lend a more strident flavour, such as is needed in Middle Eastern cookery.

Some herbs are habitually used dried and not as a substitute for fresh ones, chiefly because the bite of their flavour is reduced by drying and their pungency becomes more acceptable. Such herbs are bay, rosemary, sage and thyme, although lemon thyme is at its most delicious when fresh.

Throughout the previous chapter 'Herbs to grow' numerous ideas have been suggested for ways in which herbs may be used to titillate the palate and enhance the flavour of food. The most important way in which they are used is in long slow cooking such as in casseroles or stews when the flavours combine to pervade the whole dish. This is why the seed is often preferable to the leaf, for example dill. However, a *bouquet garni*, which appears in many recipes, is a small bunch or bouquet of mixed herbs tied together. The composition varies with the kind of dish being prepared, and it is usual to tie the little bunch to the side of the cooking utensil and remove and discard it before serving. Commercially, small muslin bags, similar to tea bags, are available; although inferior and invariable, they can be used in a similar way when fresh herbs are not forthcoming. In general, a *bouquet garni* for use in preparing poultry or game recipes might be a couple of sprigs of dried thyme, a stalk or two of fresh parsley and a bay leaf. A general *bouquet garni* for use with meat cooked slowly is a stalk or two of dried thyme, stems of fresh parsley, one of marjoram, one of dried rosemary, a bay leaf and an inch or two of celery or lovage stem. A *bouquet garni* can be small or large according to taste and for a wide variety of dishes it can be made up to individual taste from: parsley, savory, rosemary, tarragon, burnet, chervil, celery, basil, thyme and bay leaf.

Fines herbes: a mixture of chopped herbs, such as parsley, chives, tarragon and chervil, cooked in the recipe and left in when served. The term is generally used, especially on menus, to mean chopped parsley, which is the only herb added to many *omelettes aux fines herbes*.

However, there are many ways in which a small amount of herb or a combination of herbs may be used in the culinary arts. Individual choice and preference are what imaginative cooking is all about. Some traditional and popular choices are given here

Soups and broths. (Leaves and/or stalks, chopped or whole, removed after cooking or left, according to personal preference.)
Alexanders, chervil, fennel, lemon balm, marjoram, mint, parsley, sorrel, tarragon, thyme, watercress.

Casseroles and stews. (It is usual to leave these in when serving, but again the sprigs of thyme need to be removed.)
Basil, bay, borage, chives, coriander seed, dill seed, garlic, lemon balm, lovage, marjoram, mint, parsley, sage, thyme.

To serve with fish. (Use either in baking or grilling, or to marinade or include in a sauce.)
Bay, caraway, chervil, dill, fennel, lemon balm, lemon thyme, marjoram, parsley, tarragon.

To serve with meat. (Use either in roasting, grilling or cooking in an open pan or wok, or in an accompanying sauce.)
Basil, bay, caraway (seed), chervil, cumin, juniper berry, mint, parsley, rosemary, sage, savory, tarragon, thyme.

To serve with poultry and game. (Use either in roasting or grilling or cooking in an open pan or wok, or in an accompanying sauce.)
Bay, coriander, lemon balm, rosemary, sage, tarragon.

To accompany eggs. (Incorporate dried or fresh herbs in the cooking, or sprinkle on as a garnish.)
Basil, chervil, chives, coriander, dill, parsley, sorrel, tarragon, thyme.

To accompany vegetables. (Herbs must not dominate the

flavour, but traditionally decorate the finished dish. Use more freely in vegetarian cooking, especially when pasta is included as in a vegetable lasagne.)

Potatoes: (use chopped as a garnish) dill, chives, mint, parsley, savory, thyme.

Peas and other pulses: (include in cooking and remove before serving) mint, rosemary, tarragon.

Cabbage, broccoli, cauliflower: (use as an accompaniment) caraway seed, rosemary, thyme.

Tomatoes: (include in the cooking) basil, chives, tarragon.

Bland vegetables such as marrow and courgette: (include in the cooking) basil, dill, lemon balm, marjoram, savory.

To accompany salads. (Either toss in chopped and mix or sprinkle on before serving.)

Anise (stalks), caraway (seed), chives, coriander, dill, fennel, mint, parsley.

Herb vinegars. (Add to *warm* cider or wine vinegar crushed fresh herbs in a glass stoppered jar or bottle. Leave in the daylight for ten to twelve days, shaking every day. Strain well and pour the vinegar into clean bottles, adding a sprig of the fresh herb. Use a cork rather than a metal bottle top.)

Basil, bay, chervil, dill (leaves), fennel, lavender, lemon balm, majoram, mint, rosemary, savory, tarragon, thyme.

Herb butters. (Chopped leaves are worked into the butter before forming butter pats.)

Chervil, chives, garlic, marigold (petals), parsley, sage, tarragon, thyme.

Yoghurt. (Use fresh chopped leaves or the seed, and stir in according to taste.)

Anise, caraway (seed), juniper (berries), marigold (petals), marjoram, mint.

Breads. (The seed is either incorporated in the dough, or more frequently sprinkled on to the bread surface before baking.)

Anise, caraway, dill, fennel, lovage, poppy, sunflower.

Sauces. (Add chopped leaves.)

Mayonnaise: (add just before serving) chives, dill, fennel, parsley, tarragon, thyme, watercress.

Basic white or Béchamel sauce is enlivened by chopped parsley to form the popular parsley sauce to serve with fish or gammon. Other herbs to try in a similar way are: fennel or dill to serve with fish or fennel combined with mint to serve with fish or chicken; dill to serve with vegetables such as marrow or potatoes; rosemary or tarragon to serve with poultry or game, hot or cold.

Tomato sauce is improved by adding shredded basil leaves.

Herb teas or tisanes. (Fresh or dried chopped leaves infused for a few minutes make a refreshing drink, or some of them can be served cold as a 'lemonade'. Sweeten to taste with honey.)

Chamomile, dill (leaves or seed), elder (flowers), fennel, lemon balm, lemon verbena, liquorice (crushed root), marigold (petals), meadowsweet, nettle, rose (hips), vervain.

Conserves and jellies. (Both savoury and sweet condiments and jams can be flavoured with herbs. They nearly all require lemon juice or apple pulp or some setting agent, but offer a range of unusual flavours.)

Savoury: basil, mint, rosemary, sage, thyme. Sweet: bergamot, elderberry (berries), lavender (flowers), lemon balm, lemon verbena, marigold (petals), rose (petals), violet (flowers).

Fennel is a favourite herb for flavouring fish dishes.

Pot-pourri

Recipes for pot-pourri vary: some of the old ones are reliable, many more recent ones vague and some rather complicated, presenting problems and expense in acquiring the recommended extracts and essences. Essentially pot-pourri is a homogeneous mixture of dried scented flower petals and aromatic leaves together with some spices, and no single perfume should predominate. In general proportions, the most successful recipes appear to combine one part leaves to seven parts flower petals with small amounts of spices and citrus peels. Flowers with thick fleshy petals like lilies, although strongly scented, are unsuitable. Flowers and leaves need to be gathered in the middle of the day or in the afternoon when they are quite dry and free of both rain and dew, and when the blossoms are just coming to their prime. Roses ought to be picked before they are fully out, but this is a sacrifice few of us can make, and petals from red roses appear to dry better than other rose petals. Pluck the petals individually from the flowerhead and spread them out on newspaper, cloth or in a garden sieve (not plastic sheeting) in a shady place to dry. The time required to get them dry and papery to the touch varies according to the moisture content of the different kinds. Other sweet-scented flowers can be treated in the same way, in lesser quantities, but rose petals form the bulk basis of a satisfactory pot-pourri and old fashioned roses are even better. Suitable flowers to include are carnations, pinks, honeysuckle, lavender, mock orange, mignonette, stocks, sweet peas and other sweet-smelling flowers. Several of the wild herbs may be used, especially those used for strewing in days gone by, like woodruff, lady's bedstraw and clover. The aromatic leaves, without stalk, to include are those of lavender, rosemary, marjoram, verbena, southernwood, scented geraniums and sweet bay. These need to be either dried and rubbed through a fine sieve or minced and dried on paper for some hours before incorporating them in a recipe.

To prepare the citrus peel, which is usually lemon peel though some recipes call for orange peel as well, pare the fruits very finely, avoiding all the white pith. Then dry the peel in a warming drawer or put it on a baking tray in the oven when the cooking is finished and the oven has been turned off. Once dry the peel can be finely minced.

Pot-pourri, literally translated from the French, means 'rotten pot', and in the early days of pot-pourri making flowers and other plant materials were virtually pickled and kept moist. Such a 'preserve' remains richly aromatic over many years and is usually kept in closed containers, opened only infrequently, when a room is to be perfumed. This kind of pot-pourri is known as moist pot-pourri.

Dry pot-pourri is less arduous to make and is more popular today, when it is enjoyed in open bowls about the house or in pot-pourri containers with holes in the lid to allow the scented air to circulate. Dry mixtures are not so long lasting.

The art of pot-pourri making has developed and changed as new fragrant plants have been introduced to Britain's gardens through the centuries. Modern recipes can be contrived or controlled to be herby, spicy, aromatic or sweet, by blending the ingredients, but many of the basic plants remain those that were used first in Elizabethan days. Many herbs can be included, such as lavender, chamomile, bergamot, catmint, lily-of-the-valley, myrtle, mignonette, lemon balm, lemon verbena, thyme, southernwood, santolina, apple mint, pineapple sage, muscatel sage, bay, broom, marjoram, hyssop, orris root and elecampane root.

Tussie-mussies

A custom of ancient refinement was the giving of a nosegay to personages of elevated rank or profession who had to enter somewhat unsavoury buildings or mix with unclean prisoners or sick persons. These nosegays have been variously called tussie-mussie, tusmore or tussemore. They make charming little gifts and can be hung in cupboards for short-term effectiveness or just put in tiny vases on the dressing table or bedside table to sweeten the air. They can be made in various ways, usually with a rosebud as the centre piece and artemisia, lemon thyme, lavender, geranium and santolina fastened around to form a tiny Victorian posy-like bunch. Fastened with a gay ribbon or backed by a frill of paper, they are a near-useless bit of enchanting nonsense.

Herb gardens today

Today the making of a 'flowery mead' or natural area where wild flowers grow in the garden is a deliberate conservation exercise. The fashion has evolved as a cultural challenge and is not always as successful as it could be. Many of the wild plants included are northern European native herbs such as would have been brought into cultivation by monks several hundred years ago. Such 'simples' were initially collected from the fields for use, then later brought into cultivation.

An attempted reconstruction of a monastic garden in which herbs were cultivated can be seen today at Mount Grace Priory near Thirsk, North Yorkshire, administered by English Heritage. An ecclesiastical spot of singular significance where a knot garden of herbs has been created is the Museum of Garden History at St Mary's-by-Lambeth, Lambeth, London. Another London garden of ecclesiastical fame is at Fulham Palace, where an old herb garden has been reinstated.

By comparison, herb gardens today comprise sophisticated collections of plants arranged decoratively in keeping with contemporary ideas of garden planting. They may be presented as scented or nosegay gardens, in which a slightly wider range of plants is included, or they may represent physic gardens, where the emphasis is on medicinal plants.

At the Chelsea Physic Garden, London, where the Society of Apothecaries first established their garden in 1674, there is now the epitome of a physic garden devoted to worldwide medicinal plants. The original formal layout remains. A modern reconstruction of a seventeenth-century physic garden is to be found behind buildings in the bustling High Street of Petersfield, Hampshire, where to protect a plot of land from urban development a garden has been made since 1988. Protected by high walls, and arranged grid-like in period fashion, are rectangular beds in which herbs cultivated in the seventeenth century are grown. An eminent botanist, John Goodyer, lived and worked in Petersfield in the seventeenth century, so the garden is dedicated to him and is now run by the Friends of the Petersfield Garden supported by the Hampshire Gardens Trust.

Yet another fascinating physic garden has been made in the

town of Hitchin, Hertfordshire, to acknowledge the town's connection with herb growing, lavender and the pharmaceutical industries. Set to one side of the Hitchin Museum, and known as the William Ransom Physic Garden, it is roughly hexagonal in shape. Plants are collated according to their use and labels proclaim quotations from Gerard and Parkinson.

Another herb garden particularly rich in physic plants is to be seen at Chenies Manor near Rickmansworth, Hertfordshire, part of the Woburn Estates of the Duke of Bedford.

Botanic gardens

Originally the name 'physic garden' was almost synonymous with 'botanic garden', physic gardens having mainly been established in conjunction with the medical schools. As the cultivation and understanding of decorative plants increased, so collections became botanic gardens and 'physic' fell into disuse. Today most botanic gardens have at least a border for herb cultivation, but excellent places to learn are the natural order beds such as those at the Royal Botanic Gardens, Kew, and the University Botanic Garden, Oxford. There the would-be herbalist can see the relationships and botanical variances of herbs and their close relatives. At Glasgow Botanic Garden

The herb garden in the Royal Horticultural Society's garden at Wisley, Surrey.

The herb garden at Hyde Hall in Essex.

there is a good herb garden sheltered by the great glasshouse, Kibble Palace, and set out amid a maze of pathways. The Royal Botanic Garden, Edinburgh, where there has been a physic garden since the seventeenth century (moved to the present site in the nineteenth century), also has a herb garden.

At the Royal Horticultural Society's Garden, Wisley, Surrey, the herb garden has been remade to emphasise the decorative value of modern herb gardens. There are also herb gardens at the Society's gardens at Hyde Hall in Essex and Rosemoor in Devon. At Kew, a visit should be made to the Queen's Garden, where to one side of the Nosegay Garden about two hundred different plants known in the seventeenth century are collected. Not all, it can be argued, are economic plants, but the visitor will be enchanted to find a wealth of herbs and richly aromatic plants. At the University of Liverpool Botanic Garden, at Ness, Wirral, there is a peaceful herb garden known as the Ledsham Garden and also a garden for disadvantaged visitors, where herbs and aromatic plants are named in Braille. The textured foliage of such herbs as sage, santolina and borage contrasts with the silkiness of the artemisias and fennel; such herbs contribute the added enjoyment of touch in many gardens.

Collections of herbs

Particularly during the 1970s and 1980s numerous traditional herbs were sought out and brought back into commercial availability in response to the demands of natural and ethnic cuisine, pure cosmetics, alternative medicine, veterinary science and the demands of holistic lifestyle. Consequently, quite unwittingly, a vast conservation exercise was undertaken. Simultaneously, the fashion for decorative herb gardens and the consequent updating of knowledge and affirmation of identity bestowed a respectability upon herbs. No longer were they shrouded in legend as ancestral curios, the cult of cranks; they came to the forefront of both horticulture and medicine – back where they were three hundred years ago.

Representative collections were made in many gardens, both large and small. Nowadays we all have our favourites, be they in public parks, gardens sometimes open to the public, cathedral precincts or a neighbouring plot. However, the vogue for creating decorative herb gardens has undoubtedly peaked, as the plants have become more widely grown and recognised. Using herbs, respecting them and continuing to cultivate them will ensure their conservation.

The National Council for the Conservation of Plants and Gardens has, as part of its plant conservation policy, established nearly 650 living plant collections in various parts of the United Kingdom. All of them can be visited by the public at some time. Several collections include herbs, but there is no national collection of herbs *per se*. The officinal plants will be included in the appropriate generic collection, for example *Salvia officinalis* (sage) will be in the Salvia Collection, together with the decorative forms and flower garden and conservatory salvias. (A list of the relevant collections is given on pages 132–3).

However, there are some particularly good collections where plants are assembled in herb gardens. One such lovely garden, made by Lady Hanham, is at Deans Court, Wimborne, Dorset, where nearly two hundred types are grown in a spacious gravel area. Not far from there, at Cranborne Manor, Cranborne, Dorset, is a sheltered rectangular herb garden first made by the Marchioness of Salisbury in the late 1960s and still maintained. Lady Salisbury moved on to Hatfield House, Hatfield, Hertfordshire, where her herb and fragrant garden can be visited.

Across the water in Jersey, Channel Isles, is one of the

The Tudor gardens at Hatfield House in Hertfordshire include many herbs; others can be found in the nearby herb garden.

loveliest herb gardens, designed by John Brookes to replace an old rose garden at the Manor of Samarès. Now more than 150 herbs are assembled according to their principal uses: cosmetic, fragrant, culinary and medicinal.

The National Trust played a leading role in creating herb gardens at several of their properties, the majority of which remain. The first was at Sissinghurst, Cranbrook, Kent, where they took over the garden that had belonged to Vita Sackville-West. Other early ones which remain include Acorn Bank, near Appleby, Cumbria, where in the old walled garden is a remarkable collection of physic plants. At Hardwick Hall, Derbyshire, as an adjunct to the Elizabethan mansion, a large *potager* style garden was designed by Paul Miles; the inspiration for the broad idea and plan came from plasterwork on the ceiling of the house. Relating design in this manner lends an integral notion and authenticity that would otherwise have been elusive.

Another National Trust herb garden in which a *potager* type of garden has been reinstated is at Felbrigg Hall, Norfolk, where pot herbs grow profusely among the fruit trees and vegetables. Not far away at Gunby, Lincolnshire, an area within a walled garden is devoted to plants for flavouring and fragrance. Buckland Abbey in Devon has a fine National Trust herb garden.

The herb garden at the Geffrye Museum, London.

A corner of the physic garden at Michelham Priory in Sussex.

At Sulgrave Manor, the home of George Washington's ancestors, near Banbury, the Herb Society has created a herb garden adjacent to the Tudor manor house. The National Herb Centre is nearby at Banbury Road, Warmington, Warwickshire.

A number of herb gardens are associated with museums. In Southampton, Hampshire, behind the Tudor House Museum, Dr Sylvia Landsberg designed a central knot garden in 1978, with attendant contemporary features such as a chamomile seat, an arbour, an arcade or covered walk, royal beasts and a privy garden.

Another museum where a peaceful herb garden has been created amid the drone of city traffic is the Geffrye Museum, London. Sussex Past has fine herb gardens at two of its properties, Michelham Priory at Upper Dicker and Priests' House, West Hoathly. Also in Sussex, at the Weald & Downland Open Air Museum, seven period gardens contain herbs appropriate to the age of the houses they complement, from Bayleaf medieval farmstead to the nineteenth-century Whittakers Cottages.

Today herbs are cultivated on balconies in cities in the great move towards container – and temporary – gardening. Herb sales points flourish in garden centres, and many herb nurseries have delightful gardens to suggest ways in which herbs may be grown.

The following National Plant Collections ®, established by the National Council for the Conservation of Plants and Gardens, include herbs.

Eryngium
Mr J. Hodson
Myerscough College
Billsbarrow
Preston
Lancashire
PR3 0RY

Lavandula
Dr S. J. Charlesworth
Downderry Nursery
Pillar Box Lane
Hadlow
Tonbridge
Kent
TN11 9SW

Mrs J. Head
6 Church Gate
Clipston-on-the-Wolds
Keyworth
Nottinghamshire
NG12 5PA

Chris and Judy Yates
The Scented Garden
Gardens Cottage
Little Bredy
Dorchester
Dorset
DT2 9HG

Mentha
David Barrett
Pen y Braich
Cesarea
Caernarfon
Gwynedd
LL54 7RF

Ms Tracy Pearman
Iden Croft Herbs
Frittenden Road
Staplehurst
Kent
TN12 0DH

Origanum
Ms Tracy Pearman
Iden Croft Herbs
Frittenden Road
Staplehurst
Kent
TN12 0DH

Mrs S. White
Chesters Walled Garden
Chollerford
Hexham
Northumberland
NE46 4BQ

Pulmonaria
Mrs Vanessa Cook
Stillingfleet Lodge
   Nurseries
Stillingfleet
York
YO19 6HP

Rosmarinus
Dr S. J. Charlesworth
Downderry Nursery
Pillar Box Lane
Hadlow
Tonbridge
Kent
TN11 9SW

Mrs P. Thoresby
Yorkstock
Clifford Moor Road
Clifford
Wetherby
West Yorkshire
LS23 6LD

Salvia
Mr and Mrs B. D. Yeo
Pleasant View Nursery
Two Mile Oak
Near Denbury
Newton Abbot
Devon
TQ12 6DG

Tanacetum
Mr G. W. Goddard
25 Morrington Road
Chingford
London
E4 7DJ

Thymus
Mrs M. Easter
L W Plants
23 Wroxham Way
Harpenden
Hertfordshire
AL5 4PP

Mr K. A. White
Chesters Walled Garden
Chollerford
Hexham
Northumberland
NE46 4BQ

Variegated sage.

Further reading

Bown, Deni. *RHS Encyclopedia of Herbs and Their Uses.* Dorling Kindersley, 1995.

Bremness, Lesley. *Herbs.* Dorling Kindersley, 1988.

Brownlow, Margaret. *Herbs and the Fragrant Garden.* The Herb Farm, Seal, 1957.

Cooper, Guy, and Taylor, Gordon. *English Herb Gardens.* Weidenfeld & Nicolson, 1986.

Davies, Jill. *A Garden of Miracles, Herbal Remedies.* Frederick Muller, 1985.

Duff, Gail. *A Book of Pot Pourri.* Orbis, 1985.

Garland, Sarah. *The Herb and Spice Book.* Weidenfeld & Nicolson, 1979.

Garland, Sarah. *The Herb Garden.* Windward, 1984.

Gordon, Lesley. *Green Magic.* Ebury Press, 1977.

Griggs, Barbara. *Green Pharmacy.* Jill Norman & Hobhouse, 1981.

McVicar, Jekka. *Jekka's Complete Herb Book.* Kyle Cathie, 1994.

Sanecki, Kay N. *The Complete Book of Herbs.* Macdonald, 1974.

Sanecki, Kay N. *The Book of Herbs.* Apple Press, 1985.

Sanecki, Kay N. *The History of the English Herb Garden.* Ward Lock, 1992.

Stuart, Malcolm (editor). *The Encyclopedia of Herbs and Herbalism.* Orbis, 1979.

Index

Page numbers in italic refer to illustrations.

Acorn Bank 129
Agrimony 25
Alchemilla 25
Alecost 26
Alexanders 26
Allium 53
Allspice 26
Angelica 27, *27*
Anise 28
Artemisia 86, 105, 109, *109*, 117
Balm 31, 68, *69*
Basil 29, *29*
Bay 30, *30*
Bee balm 31
Bergamot 31
Betony 31
Bistort 31, *32*
Bitterwort 54
Black lovage 26
Bloodroot 32
Bog myrtle 33
Borage 33, *34*, 127
Botanic gardens 126-7
Bouquet garni 78, 119
Brookes, John 129
Brooklime 34
Buckland Abbey 129
Burdock 35
Button snakeroot 35
Camphor plant 36
Caraway 36
Catmint 36
Catnep 36
Centaury 37
Chamomile 37, *38*, 131
Cheeses 75
Chelsea Physic Garden 125
Chenies Manor 126
Chervil 39
Chicory 39, *39*
Chives 40
Christmas rose 40
Church steeples 25
Clary 41

Coltsfoot 41
Comfrey 41
Conserves 122
Containers 16-17
Cooking 119-22
Coriander 42
Corn salad 43
Costmary 26
Cotton lavender 68
Coughwort 41
Cowslip 43
Cranborne Manor 128
Cumin 44
Curry plant 44, *44*
Dandelion 45
Deans Court garden 128
Dewcup 25
Dill 45
Disadvantaged, gardens for 127
Drying herbs 21-4
Dyer's woad 116
Easter ledges 31, *32*
Edinburgh: Royal Botanic Garden 127
Elder 46
Elecampane 47, *47*
English mace 74
Eryngo 101
Evening primrose 48
Felbrigg Hall 129
Fennel 49, *49*, *122*, 127
Fenugreek 50
Feverfew 51, *51*
Foxglove 52, *52*
Freezing herbs 24
Fulham Palace 125
Garlic 53
Geffrye Museum *130*, 131
Gentian 54
Germander 54
Glasgow Botanic Garden 126
Goat's rue 55

Good King Henry 55, *55*
Goosefoot 55
Greek hayseed 50
Ground ivy 56
Gunby Hall 129
Hanham, Lady 128
Hardwick Hall 129
Harvesting 18-20
Hatfield House 128, *129*
Hellebore 40
Henbane 56
Herb butter 121
Herb gardens 125-31
Herb Society *13*, 131
Herb vinegar 121
Hitchin: William Ransom Physic Garden 126
Horehound 57, *57*
Horse cress 34
Horseradish 58, *58*
Hound's tongue 59
Houseleek 59, *60*
Hyde Hall, RHS garden 127, *127*
Hyssop 61, *61*
Indian physic 62
Iris 89
Ivy 62, *62*
Jacob's ladder 63
Juniper 63
Kew: Royal Botanic Gardens 126, 127
Knitbone 41
Lad's love 105
Lady's mantle 25
Lambeth: St Mary's 125
Lamb's lettuce 43
Landsberg, Dr Sylvia 131
Lavender 64-7, *64*
Lavender cotton 68
Lemon balm 68, *69*
Lemon verbena 69

Licorice 70
Lily-of-the-valley 71
Lime 71
Liverpool, University of *15*, 127
Loosestrife 72
Lovage 72, *73*
Lungwort 73
Mace 74
Mallow 75, *75*
Marigold 76, *76*
Marjoram 77, *77, 78*
Meadowsweet 79, *79*
Melilot 80
Michelham Priory *130*, 131
Mignonette 80
Miles, Paul 129
Mint 81-5, *81, 82, 84*
Monarda 31
Monastic gardens 125
Motherwort 85
Mount Grace Priory 125
Mugwort 86
Mullein 86
Museum of Garden History 125
Myrtle 87
Nasturtium *11*, 87, *88*
National Collections 111, 128, 132-3
National Council for the Conservation of Plants and Gardens 128, 132-3
National Herb Centre 6, 131
National Trust 129
Ness Botanic Garden *15*, 127
Nettle 88
Nosegay gardens 125, 126
Old man 105
Opium poppy 89

Orris 89
Oswego tea 31
Oxford: University Botanic Garden 126
Parsley *9*, 90, *90*
Parsley, Chinese 44
Periwinkle 91
Petersfield herb garden 125
Physic gardens 125-6
Poppy 89
Pot-pourri 26, 27, 67, 79, 90, 92, 94, 117, 118, 123-4
Priest House *4*, 131
Purslane 92
Queen's Garden, Kew 127
Rampion 92
Renovation 10
Rose 92
Rosemary 93, *94*
Rosemoor, RHS garden *14*, 127
Royal Horticultural Society *14*, 127
Rue 94, *95*
Saffron 96
Sage *19*, 96-100, *97, 98, 99*, 127, 128, *133*
Salad burnet 100
Salisbury, Marchioness of 128
Samarès, Manor of 129
Santolina 68, 127
Sauces 121
Savory 100, *101*
Scented gardens 125
Sea holly 101
Selfheal 102
Sissinghurst 129
Snakeroot 31, *32*
Soapwort 102, *102*
Society of Apothecaries 125
Soil condition 7-8

Solomon's seal 103, *103*
Sorrel 104, *104*
Soups 120
Southampton: Tudor House Museum 131
Southernwood 105
Spearmint 83
Storing herbs 24
Succory 39, *39*
Sulgrave Manor *13*, 131
Sunflower 105, *106*
Sweet basil 29, *29*
Sweet Cicely 107, *107*
Sweet gale 33
Tansy 108, *108*
Tarragon 109, *109*
Thyme 14, 110-12, *110, 111*
Tisanes 122
Tudor House Museum 131
Tussie-mussies 124
Valerian 112, *113*
Veratrum 113
Verbascum 86
Verbena 69
Vervain 114
Violet 114
Weald & Downland Open Air Museum 131
Welsh onion 115, *115*
Wimborne: Deans Court 128
Wintergreen 116
Wisley: RHS Garden *17*, *126*, 127
Woad 116
Wood betony 31
Woodruff 116, *117*
Wormwood 117
Yarrow 118
Yoghurt 121